TABLE OF CONTENTS

ACRONYMS

ACSOR	Afghan Center for Socio-Economic and Opinion
AFPAK	Afghanistan-Pakistan
ALP	Afghanistan Local Police
ANA	Afghanistan National Army
ANP	Afghanistan National Police
ANSF	Afghan National Security Forces
APO	Assistant Political Officer
ASOP	Afghanistan Social Outreach Program
CFSOCC-A	Combined Forces Special Operations Component Command
COG	Center of Gravity
COIN	Counterinsurgency
CORDS	Civil Operations and Revolutionary Development Support
DAT	District Augmentation Team
DCC	District Community Council
DGOV	District Governor
DLO	District Liaison Officer
DoS	Department of State
FATA	Federally Administered Tribal Areas
FARC	Fuerzas Armadas Revolucionarias de Colombia
FM	Field Manual
GoA	Government of Afghanistan
GVN	Government of Vietnam
IDLG	Independent Directorate for Local Governance

ISAF	International Security Assistance Forces
LEDSP	Leader Development Education for Sustained Peace
LEP	Law Enforcement Professional
LLO	Logical Lines of Operations
MOE	Measure of Effectiveness
MoI	Ministry of Interior
MOP	Measure of Performance
MRRD	Ministry of Rural Rehabilitation and Development
NATO	North Atlantic Treaty Organization
NDS	National Directorate of Security
NWFI	North Western Frontier of India
NWFP	North Western Frontier Province
OCO	Office of Civil Operations
PDPA	People's Democratic Party of Afghanistan
PO	Political Officer
PRT	Provincial Reconstruction Team
SFAT	Security Forces Assistance Team
VC	Viet Cong
VCI	Viet Cong Irregular
USAID	United States Agency for International Development
VSO	Village Stability Operations

ILLUSTRATIONS

TABLES

CHAPTER 1

INTRODUCTION

> Society in every state is a blessing, but government, even in its best state, is but a necessary evil; in its worst state an intolerable one.
> —Thomas Paine, *Common Sense*

On 2 May 2012 the President of the United States, Barack Obama, and Afghan President Hamid Karzai further advanced their efforts and negotiations regarding the future of The Islamic Republic of Afghanistan by signing the "Enduring Strategic Partnership Agreement" between their two countries. The agreement solidified and developed aspects of the 2010 London and Kabul Conferences as well as the 2011 Bonn Conference. Amongst the eight provisions listed in the agreement, a strong confirmation of the commitment of both countries was made to "Strengthening Afghanistan's Institutions and Governance" (The White House 2012). After twelve years of close partnership with the Afghan Government and a commitment by the United States to transition out by 2014, a path for self-reliance for their own security, economic development and governance becomes even more critical for the leaders and the people of Afghanistan.

According to the U.S. Army and Marine Corps Counterinsurgency Field Manual, Logical Lines of Operation (LLOs) which are conceptual topics that are used to synchronize operations against an enemy that hides amongst the populace, are closely related to the success or failure of counterinsurgency efforts (Department of the Army 2007, 154). Some of the primary and more commonly use LLOs are: (1) Combat Operations/Civil Security Operations, (2) Host Nation Security Forces, (3) Essential

Services, (4) Governance, and (5) Economic Development. While all the LLOs reinforce the success of one other, the concept of governance is a critical aspect of the progress of stability as a focal point of combating an insurgency. The ability of a government to provide an effective governance mechanism is a key element especially in regions like the Eastern area of the Paktika Province in the Eastern Afghanistan, which is affected by its border with the Federally Administered Tribal Areas (FATA) of Pakistan (DAT-Bermal 2012). While these LLOs including governance are not a predetermined winning formula or are to be used in any specific sequence in a counterinsurgency, they do reflect a basic theme within the stability framework in a population-centric conflict.

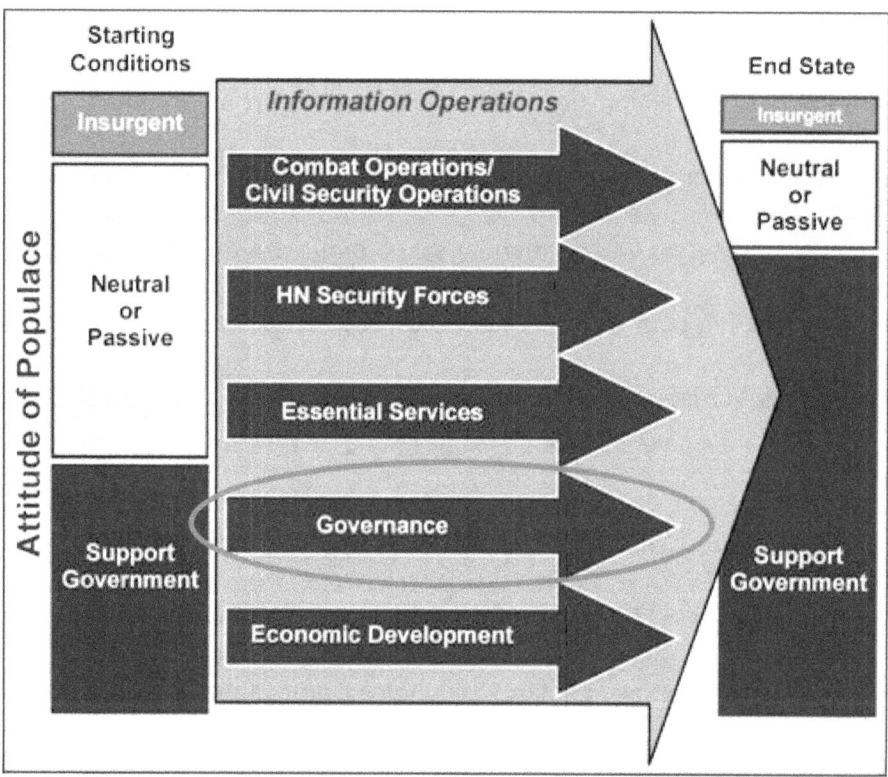

Figure 1.   Example of logical lines of operations for a counterinsurgency

Source: Headquarters, Department of the Army, Field Manual (FM) 3-24, *Counterinsurgency* (Washington, DC: Government Printing Office, 2006), 155.

The Government of Afghanistan continues to attempt to manage a critical time in their development of district level governments along the Eastern border region. Based on the challenges and failures constantly seen at the district and village levels, stemming from what can be described as an inherent "acceptable corruption" and ineptness at the provincial-level, a unilateral effort by the International Security Assistance Force (ISAF) remains at the forefront of any stability in many areas of this region. This corruption is often characterized by graft that exploits an inefficient government system whose chief goals are providing shelter, food, or other items necessary for daily existence (Casper 2012). While this acceptance is definitely "unofficial" its effects are viewed as if they were. Corruption flourishes throughout the Afghanistan government, especially at the lower levels, as billions of dollars from assisting nations have flooded one of the poorest countries in the world and now must take some of the responsibility. While no one ever really accepts corruption, the collective dismissal of lower-level corruption by the government of Afghanistan bleeds over onto coalition forces' efforts and perpetuates a system of governance powered by bribes, nepotism, and willful ignorance of laws and procedures especially at the district level. This promotes a commonly held belief of Afghans and coalition personnel that "this is just the way it is done in Afghanistan." As a result of the dishonesty by local government actors, coalition forces are finding little assistance from them and on many occasions even resistance from the government and military leadership of Afghanistan in these rural areas to update systems and ideology on improving these systems. While partial success has been achieved with the joint and mutually supported efforts of military forces, non-governmental agencies, and international government agencies, true development of a functional and effective Afghan local government mechanism is still far from being achieved (Kaim 2011).

The purpose of this study is to better understand what challenges faced selected counterinsurgency efforts, including and focusing in rural Eastern Afghanistan, and to recommend/propose efforts to improve their ability to govern. The relevance brought out by this question is based on the continuing combat, insurgency, and search for stability as part of ongoing operations in the Eastern region of the Paktika Province and its border with Pakistan; therefore making it the primary focus of the analysis. The time frame selected is the aftermath of the 2010 surge of ISAF and United States troops, which had the purpose of assisting the counterinsurgency (COIN) mission. Districts such as Bermal, Shkin, and Sarobi, which are usually not mentioned in studies or references, are essential to the advancement of progress in the Paktika Province, due to their proximity to the permeable Afghanistan/Pakistan border. This permeability allows contraband, insurgent movement, and more importantly the South Waziristan influence of Eastern Afghanistan into an already troubled region. One of the major reasons for the emphasis on Eastern Afghanistan is the critical importance this region plays in the counterinsurgency efforts of coalition forces in Afghanistan.

Since the formation of the *Tehrik-i-Taliban Pakistan* (TTP) in December 2007, an umbrella organization uniting *Taliban* militant groups in Pakistan, nearly 40 Taliban groups have joined its cause up to this point. These factions/groups continue to operate against US and the North Atlantic Treaty Organization (NATO) forces using the city of Miram Shah in North Waziristan, as their headquarters (Mahsud 2010). The danger that these factions represent are a direct concern for the US as "our core goal of disrupting,

4

dismantling, and defeating al-Qa'ida and preventing Afghanistan from ever being a safe haven again will be central to this effort" (Department of Defense 2012).

While the emphasis of the analysis remains at the district level government and its challenges, however the role of the Afghanistan National Security Forces (ANSF) is critical. Therefore, the influence and effects of the Afghanistan National Army (ANA), the Afghanistan National Police (ANP), the Afghanistan Local Police (ALP) and the National Directorate of Security (NDS), are topics that require and are given attention in this study to further understand both the positive and negative aspects of the development of this specific region.

Figure 2.   Current political map of Afghanistan

Source: 411th Engineer Brigade Brief, http://411enbde.net/G2//training/Afghanistan-Threat (accessed 20 April 2013).

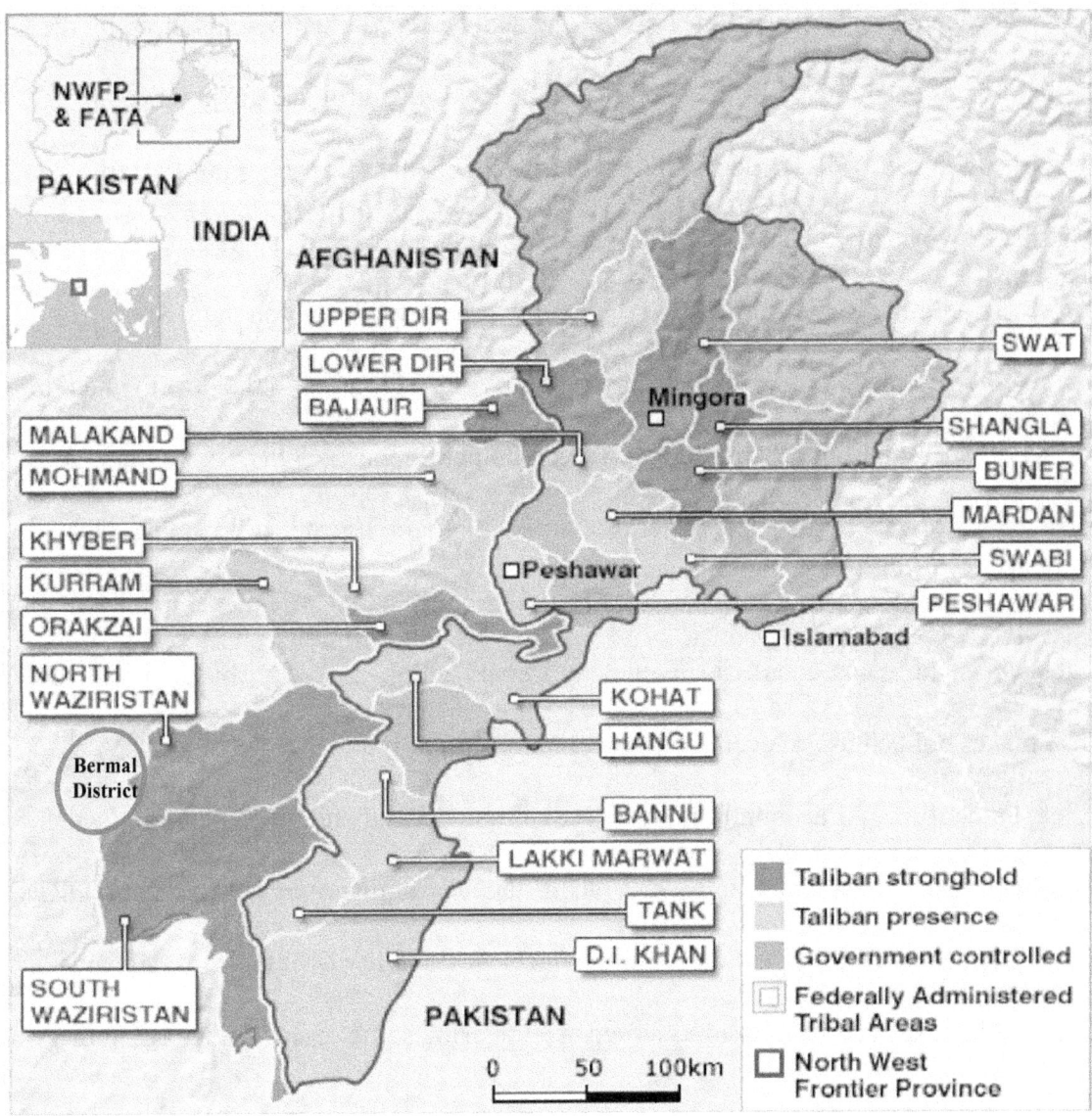

Figure 3.   Taliban influence in the FATA (Afghanistan-Pakistan Border)

Source: Naval Postgraduate School (NPS), Program for Culture & Conflict Studies, Afghanistan Administrative Divisions, Afghanistan Tribal Map, 15 November 2011, www.nps.edu/programs/ccs (accessed 21 April 2013).

Historical Case Study

To provide a regionally relevant example and background to understand the

current challenges of governance and stability and its effectiveness in Eastern Paktika province, a similar historical case is used. The analysis used the problems faced by the British forces encountered as they addressed the lack of control and governance in Waziristan in the 1930s (Bruce 1938, 7). This in fact is the same region of Eastern Paktika Province that is the focus of this contemporary study and analysis.

In addition to the study of Waziristan, this study will focus on the US involvement in the Vietnam War. From the "agrovilles" Program to the development of the Civil Operations and Revolutionary Development Support (CORDS) program, and their efforts to govern, develop and secure South Vietnam. It is no surprise that the US involvement in Vietnam from 1962 to 1972 is also a critical historical example the author cites when addressing counterinsurgency topics and lessons learned. This analysis will also makes pointed use of events, strategies and learning points written about the Vietnam conflict to draw similarities, objectives and desired end states between this conflict and the attempt at stability in Afghanistan. The comparison between the CORDS program used in Vietnam and the current strategy for stability operations in Afghanistan will put context to current attempts aimed at addressing some of the challenges in the Eastern Paktika districts.

The experience of the British in Waziristan in the 1900s, as well as the American experience in Vietnam, provided valuable background to COIN efforts in modern times. While the ultimate results of the campaigns may not have been successful, these COIN efforts were successful in providing a template of lessons learned and in some cases success on a limited scale. By demonstrating some of the similar programs in relations to the delivery of governance, along with their results, this analysis will evaluate the potential strengths and shortcomings of the current approach to Eastern Paktika.

Contemporary Case Study

The contemporary local government that the author will be view for this analysis, is the Bermal District, in the Paktika Province of Eastern Afghanistan, with a primary focus on the timeframe of April 2011 to May 2012. A supporting comparison will be made using adjacent districts and communities within the same province (Sarobi District and Shkin District [unofficial]), which in many cases have a direct impact on Bermal. Utilizing published materials, including United States Government political and military reports on Afghan progress, Government of Afghanistan reports, along with interviews of interagency elements and Bermal District Augmentation Team reports, results will address the challenges and progress that the Bermal District has experienced.

The Aim of this Study

This study has three goals: to inform the reader of ongoing stability operations and its challenges; to analyze the methodology being applied to measure progress; and to make recommendations on improving the evaluation of governance in the Bermal district within the Paktika Province. As part of these goals, this analysis also focuses to bring clarity to the difficulties facing the district governments in Eastern Paktika in legitimizing their actions and current status. As the position of the local government and its representatives are under scrutiny in this region, commonly referred to as Waziristan by the inhabitants. The second goal of this report is to compare the current Measures of Effectiveness (MOE) as stated by the Afghan Government in their very general progress reports, as they are compared to contradictory reports and firsthand accounts coming from on-the-ground sources regarding this border region. These discrepancies will be argued extend from the lack of involvement and presence of the Government of

Afghanistan (GoA) in many of these rural and troubled areas (districts). This lack of governance creates a vicious cycle: poor security prevents any significant efforts at development, which in turn leads to a lack of support for the government by the village and tribal leaders. The final goal of this report is to provide a better understanding of the Waziristan region and a possible mythology to proceed and address the difficult cultural, ethnic, and tribal dynamics that continue to hamper GoA and international assistance stability efforts in that region.

Definition of Terms

To ensure clarity and avoid confusion through the text, it is critical that some of the key terms and concepts used, such as "governance," "stability," "effectiveness" and "counterinsurgency," be defined. While it may seem unnecessary to define the terms "insurgency" and "counterinsurgency" after twelve years of involvement in the Afghanistan conflict; however, it is useful for academic reasons, and also to ensure that when other terms are associated with this theme, the correct frame is visualized. The U.S. Army and Marine Corps Field Manual FM 3-24: *Counterinsurgency* defines insurgency as "an organized movement aimed at the overthrow of a constituted *government* through the use of subversion and armed conflict." The key word in this definition is "government," which is the basis of the analysis in this study. According to FM 3-24, counterinsurgency (COIN), using once again FM 3-24, also focuses on "government"; as it highlights in its definition of "the military, paramilitary, political, economical, psychological, and civic-action taken by a *government* to defeat an insurgency" (Department of the Army 2007, 2).

Within the theme of counterinsurgency and stability additional key terms needed to be defined. Key terms such as LLO, as depicted in figure 1 represent the doctrinal concept used by the United States Army to assist and guide the host nation government and the armed forces commander in how to engage the insurgency. The desired objectives used to engage an insurgency are not written in stone, but have a common theme of positively affecting the population, as they are the Center of Gravity (COG). Some of the primarily used LLOs to establish government legitimacy and maintain the focus on the population are: Combat Operations/Civil Security Operations, Host Nation Security Forces, Essential Services, Governance, and Economic Development (Department of the Army 2007, 155). As part of a 2006 conference in Washington D.C., Dr. David Kilcullen (counter-insurgency advisor to General David Petraeus in 2007-2008) presented his theme of the "Three Pillars of Counterinsurgency," which further narrows down these LLOs. Dr. Kilcullen's simplification and combination of the LLOs into the three main topics: Security, Political (Governance), and Economic (Development), reinforced the importance of the functional and effective government theme.

To support this thesis the author uses relevant government reports and status updates for the progress of the local government of Bermal are presented to support this thesis. Also extensive and as well as deliberate firsthand accounts from the Bermal District Augmentation Team (DAT) and other similar teams within this area of operations to support this thesis, and to assist in confirming or denying the validity of these reports.

It is for this reason that defining and identifying the role of the DAT is critical. A DAT is an element most often than made up of a two men team, and occasionally a solo member working in direct support of the Village Stability Platforms, under the umbrella of Village Stability Operations (VSO) of the Combined Forces Special Operations Component Command–Afghanistan (CFSOCC-A). As US Military members, their main task is to provide the link between the villages and ALP initiative to their local district government, by assisting with the development of these communities. The assistance comes in the form of aiding the district government to identify the needs of the community and making every effort to meet them. It also provides another pathway for the district to reach provincial visibility, pushing (energizing) the provincial leadership to acknowledge and provide some sort of resolution to their request. With dozens of DATs operating in various key provinces and districts through Afghanistan, and conducting several hundred key leader engagements every year with village, tribal, and local government leaders, they have become a critical aspect of the operational picture for coalition forces at the local, regional and national-level (DAT-Bermal 2012).

The last two terms to be defined are "stable governance" and, even more important, "effective governance." The efforts of the international coalition and their governments are based on the accomplishment of the final end state derived from these two terms. FM 3-07, the United States Army Manual that covers stability operations, describes stable governance as "the legitimate system of political representation at the national, provincial and local level, which provides accountability of leadership and institutions promoted, stewardship of state resources promoted, civic participation and empowerment encouraged, and a provision of government services supported to determine its success" (Department of the Army 2008, 1-87 to 1-89). By comparison, FM

3-07 describes effective governance as "the actual ability of the government at any level, to provide the population with essential services" (Department of the Army 2008, 3-52).

Limitations

This thesis recognizes the width and breath of the COIN and stability efforts that have been occurring in Afghanistan following the removal of the *Taliban* government in 2001. The United States has been directly involved in stability efforts for over eleven years; while the Afghan people have faced decades of instability. The challenges of establishing governance in Afghanistan have been the subject of numerous studies and reports. This thesis will add to the body of knowledge but on a smaller scale: focusing on a single district. These self-imposed limitations will narrow the issue to a more manageable topic. In an effort to provide new information and make a contribution to the vast amount of knowledge already covered in other published works, the analysis focuses on the governance efforts from April 2011until April 2012, coinciding with the aftermath of the 2010 surge of an additional 30,000 U.S. troops into Afghanistan, to assist the approximately 80,000 that were already in the theater of operations. It will also focus mainly on governance, with the understanding that in many instances other LLOs such as security and development supplement or work in combination with the primary topic. Finally, due to the extensive size of the area of operations (AO), the focus will remain on the Eastern Paktika Province, and the districts already mentioned. While this is a very small and specific region of the country of Afghanistan, its similarities with many rural secluded areas and districts throughout other parts of Afghanistan is a valid and legitimate indicator of the types of challenges faced by the districts and provinces around the country. Furthermore, the lessons learned from this volatile area can be applied to other unstable areas that are lacking sufficient governance.

Thesis Structure

The thesis structure follows a five chapter model: the introduction; defining the problem and questions to be answered, chapter 2; the literary review, chapter 3; is the research methodology used, with the analysis and conclusion developing in chapters 4 and 5. The current chapter introduces the theme of the discussion and subsequent questions to be analyzed. Chapter 2 will outline a general review of the literature and sources of information gathered regarding the topics of effective use of counterinsurgency and its LLOs, then exploring the current status of the topic LLO which is "governance," in the counterinsurgency efforts in Afghanistan. The chapter concludes with a more detailed view of the literature, which focuses on the challenges of governance in the critical province of Paktika, Afghanistan and more specifically the Eastern region of such province. Chapter 3 presents the methodology used to analyze the current status being reported, the challenges being seen at the ground-level, the distinction between the two, and the impact on the evaluation of governance efforts. Another aspect of the methodology uses historical cases to determine the ideology behind the current strategies and their results and eventual relevance in more contemporary situation. Chapter 4 presents the review of the current status of governance in Eastern Paktika Province noting its successes, describing its challenges but more importantly analyzing the possible causes for successes, challenges, failures, and the reported way ahead, based on official reports. Finally, chapter 5 summarizes the thesis with current status of region in an effort to create a basic understanding of the current status of governance in the region, along with the proposed recommendations to address some of the key remaining challenges in the near future, given that President Obama has pledged to pull out (most) U.S. troops by 2014. The other major end state for this study is to contribute a compilation of lessons learned in regards to the effectiveness of national- and provincial-level governance strategy in some of the most rural districts in Afghanistan. The analysis and comparison of strategies and programs focused on government efficiency, which in turn ties in the other LLOs, is intended to assist any efforts now and in the future in developing a legitimate, functional, and effective governance mechanism.

CHAPTER 2

LITERATURE REVIEW

Where government actions become inept and corrupt, the urban guerilla should not hesitate to step in and show that he opposes the government, and thus gain popular sympathy.
—Carlos Marighella, *For the Liberation of Brazil*

A Broad View of Counterinsurgency

Prior to the analysis of this subject, the initial view of the research looks at the

broad aspect of insurgencies and counterinsurgency. Subsequently, the view is narrowed

to Afghanistan and its history of poverty, illiteracy, conflict, foreign invasions, control

and development of the current rural (district and village level) political status. Finally,

the study focuses on the theme in question: the current challenges in achieving

effectiveness of governance in the Eastern region of the Paktika Province of Afghanistan.

Over the last 50 years, with an unprecedented explosion of the information era

and the birth of globalization, the international community has witnessed the

development of a theater of war unlike the historical great battles of Napoleon and

Frederick the Great. The birth of insurgencies, insurrections, and their nemesis,

counterinsurgency, date to these same periods and even before. However, the modern

information, communication, and economic links in today's world require the use of

modern day counterinsurgency techniques as the possible antidote for any small state,

terrorist organization or radical elements led conflict. The effective use of the antidote of

counterinsurgency becomes a critical priority as many of these organizations and groups

continue to challenge and test the historically "superior" military and economic powers of the world. In order to understand the ongoing counterinsurgency efforts in Afghanistan, it is necessary to reflect and understand that insurgencies are rebellions against instituted governments (Department of the Army 2006, 2). Any rebellion's fight to overthrow an unjust and oppressive government or dislodge a fair, just and legitimate one is secondary for the purpose of this analysis. The key point is that in either case the insurgents must have or must obtain the support of the population or they will fail. In most historical examples, the insurgent or counterinsurgent side that identifies and controls the COG (support of the population), definitely tips the scale in his favor for gaining the final victory. For a counterinsurgency to be successful it must first revisit the military blunders that have lost counterinsurgents the fight in past conflicts. The focus however must be on the political successes and failures that drive the historical counterinsurgency effort such as: China in the 1930s to the 1940s, Vietnam fighting the French from 1945 to 1954, and the US from 1962 to 1972, Cuba from 1956 to 1959, and even Spain during the Peninsula War from 1808 to 1814 (Joes 2010, 2).

Doctrinal Counterinsurgency

This analysis makes frequent reference to US counterinsurgency doctrine, with direct quotes along with its concepts and theories throughout the discussion. The primary source of the detailed information comes from Field Manual, FM 3-24 the United States Army and Marine Corps: *Counterinsurgency*. The use of FM 3-24 and FM 3-07 (*Stability Operations*) and their counterinsurgency approaches, concept of LLOs and definitions of "stability" and "effectiveness" in reference to governance create part of that broad base understanding of counterinsurgency. This base is a requirement to understand the theories and strategies used over the last several years to address insurgency and stability issues in the Iraq Theater of Operations and Afghanistan. Another publication relevant to the continuation of stability efforts in Afghanistan but used very sparingly through the document is the "Guiding Principles for Stabilization and Reconstruction" produced by the United States Institute for Peace. The sparse use of this source of information is due to its non-doctrinal certification and not being a government endorsed publication. However, its use by civilian entities is of great importance and it is treated as a strategic tool by many non-governmental agencies currently operating in Afghanistan. Therefore the author gives it careful consideration and uses it sparingly in this study.

Continuing with the broad view of insurgency and counterinsurgency, the review and use of literature on COIN efforts in Vietnam by the United States revealed trends of strategies and methodologies that remained in use during the recent conflicts in Iraq and Afghanistan. While military victories are desired and key for both sides, the government plays the largest and most important role in the ability or lack thereof to gain and maintain popular support (Moyar 2007, 9). The role of the government and its efforts or the lack of these efforts to support the population with basic security needs and services, can open or close the door to an insurgency as it did in the case of the Vietnam conflict. Knowing that one of the greatest obstacles for the Viet Cong (VC) movement was the political presence by the Government of Vietnam (GVN) officials in the villages/hamlets, the VC engaged in a campaign to discourage government involvement in certain areas. The VC targeted the government and its representatives, by coercion them, corrupting them and as a final recourse by kidnapping them or assassinating them. This proved to be an effective dissuasion campaign and resulted in the absence of the Vietnamese officials in some provinces around the country. In the 1950s and 1960s, due to the lack of influence and presence by the GVN, a Viet Cong shadow government known as "cadres" filled in the void. An effective dissuasion campaign by the VC resulted in the absence of the Vietnamese officials in some provinces around the country. Thus, an envelopment of these areas by the VC became complete. In May 1967, in response to these insurgent tactics President Johnson established the CORDS program with the intent to pacify these regions (Moyar 2007, 14).

The Graveyard of Empires

Called "The Graveyard of Empires" (Jones, 2009), Afghanistan has seen a multitude of foreign forces come and go. The British Empire sent troops to Afghanistan several times in the 1800s, only to meet with disaster, defeat, and retreat. During three different conflicts (Anglo-Afghan Wars) in 1839-42, in 1878-80 and then again in 1919 British forces intended to subjugate Afghanistan in order to advance their control over the then Northwest Region of India and Afghanistan proper to influence and oppose the Russian interest in the area (Britannica 2012). Unable to maintain substantial control over the central Afghanistan Government, the British focus was redirected to the Northwest frontier region of India (Waziristan). However, this tribal territory separating modern day Pakistan and Afghanistan has always been a main point of friction and problems. The British decision to use the "Close Border" system, sometimes called "the policy of nonintervention," allowed a continual state of anarchy and chaos in the area, allowing for outlaws and raiding gangs to find sanctuary. This lack of order failed to provide the primary test and requisite of looking out for the welfare of the tribes and subsequently losing any support for the policies dictated but not enforced (Bruce 1938, 3). It could be argued that the attraction to a nonintervention policy in this region for the British Empire and the Indian Government was to avoid operating in a region known for its punishing mountainous, and hard to supply terrain, and its lack of savvy in how to govern or control the inhabitants. Both of these main issues are discussed in further detailed during the analysis in chapter 4.

In April 1978 the People's Democratic Party of Afghanistan (PDPA) assassinated Afghanistan's leader Daud Khan and mounted a military coup to take control of the government of Afghanistan. This action was met with immediate opposition by much of the population and included armed revolts. These were followed by a mass desertion of members of the armed forces to join the resistance. In December 1979 the Soviet Union unwilling to allow the failure of the communist takeover that they supported, invaded Afghanistan, taking immediate control of the main cities right away (Grau 1996, 15). For more than a decade, the Soviet military forces in Afghanistan fought against counterinsurgents, but could not defeat them. Why? "They were unable to seal the border with Pakistan and Iran to prevent the *Mujahideen* resupply of their forces. Afghanistan is a country of strong beliefs and traditions and the population opposed the Soviets and the hostile communist ideology of the government of Afghanistan" (Grau 1996, 101).

The Current Status of Eastern Paktika

The analysis draws situational awareness and knowledge from national strategic documents and briefs that provide a guideline as to the direction of possible courses of action for continual development of the Afghanistan Government at all levels. In his 20 March 2012 testimony to congress on the status of stability operations in Afghanistan, General John Allen (Commander of ISAF and U.S. troops) spoke of the overall security improvements in Afghanistan. As he explained to the panel congressional committee, the

Afghan Security Forces were progressing rapidly with increasing numbers of personnel trained and facilitating other major factors of the country's stability. However, during the same testimony, when asked by Senator John McCain (R-Arizona) about the delayed transition of efforts in Southern Afghanistan to the next priority region, Eastern Afghanistan, General Allen explained that transitioning to the Eastern region of the country, including the location chosen for this analysis, might be delayed to ensure no capabilities and momentum was lost in the South (U.S. Senate 2012). The significance of this delay ties in directly with the known Taliban factions operating out of North Waziristan and their continual use of the region for insurgent operations, as addressed previously in chapter 1.

Using various US and Afghan Government sources and reports, the analysis sets a base understanding of what is being reported in regards to status of Afghan government and development capabilities. These reports are the basis for many decisions being made to proceed with programs, and initiatives within the Afghanistan plan of development, which directly affect the Eastern Paktika region. The review of official government documents such as: The Afghanistan National Development Strategy, The Surveys of the Afghan People from 2008 to 2011 produced by The Asia Foundation, and The Afghan Center for Socio-Economic and Opinion Research (ACSOR), assists the analysis by providing valuable current popular sentiment and information. Critical information gathered from these sources are: a guide to the Government of Afghanistan's priorities and plans for their continual development, the ACSOR surveys provide the results of conducted surveys of Afghan citizens and their input into security, reconstruction, peace, development, and most important for the purpose of this thesis, governance.

In the Afghanistan People Survey of 2011, the Asia Foundation reported that; "Four-fifths of respondents (80 percent) assess their provincial government positively, including 29 percent who say that the provincial government is doing a very good job. Positive assessments of provincial governments have been gradually rising since 2008 (from 74 percent in 2008 to 75 percent in 2009, 78 percent in 2010 and 80 percent in 2011, which is equal to the highest figure recorded in 2007 (80 percent)" (Rennie 2011, 79).

At first glance the percentages presented appear very promising; however, the details of the sources of the data must play a bigger role in the acceptance of the data before generalizing and assuming that it is reflects all areas in Afghanistan. The percentages above were taken based on 6348 people surveyed nationwide. If divided by the 398 districts within the 34 provinces that make up the country of Afghanistan, the results reflect an average of 16 people per district surveyed (Central Intelligence Agency 2013). With a population reported in excess of 88,000 residents in the Bermal District, 16 people would represent only 0.02 percent of the district (MRRD 2004), which may not be a sufficient sample size to draw any conclusions.

The focal point for this study is the rural and secluded region of the Bermal District in the Eastern Paktika Province of Afghanistan. Addressing this specific region it is necessary to gather and include first hand (primary source) data, which is limited to a narrow window of time, covering from April 2011 to April 2012. This time limitation assists the accuracy and relevance of specific reports and information gathered from coalition forces (to include the author), local Afghan civilians, personnel from United States Government agencies along with non-governmental agencies.

In April 2011, as part of an Afghan Ministry of Interior (MoI) initiative under the umbrella of the CFSOCC-A and more specifically under VSO, the author begins his engagement of the district level governance and development issues for the Bermal District in Eastern Paktika. During this period the Bermal district was under the assessment and mentorship of a DAT in conjunction with a special operations team, a coalition forces infantry company, and was coached and supported long distance by the United States Department of State (DoS), the Paktika Provincial Reconstruction Team (PRT) and United States Agency for International Development (USAID) personnel at the provincial level. All elements conducted daily engagements at the various levels of government within the province, district and villages, producing daily status reports on security, governance and development issues in the district and nearby areas. The interviews of these personnel and the unclassified data and information they witnessed and provided for this study forms a large part of the current known status of the Bermal district and its surrounding areas.

Due to their positions, location and access to local government leaders and systems, these Bermal primary sources were privy to public government reports. Reports which provided a view of funds allocation, project priorities and government official grievances, along with the accompanying requests and issues. Due to the inherent relationship between the district leadership and the ANP and the government-required coordination with the ANA in the region, the mentoring coalition teams, or the Security Forces Assistance Teams (SFAT) as they are called, assigned to the Bermal district during that time were also part of the interviewees asked to participate in the analysis. For the ANP, their foreign Law Enforcement Professional (LEP) mentor provided concurring data as he coordinated with the DAT on a daily basis for local security, police and government issues. For their part, the ANA mentors, a team of three senior United States officers and non-commissioned officers, provided the host nation perspective for security, governance and stability for the region.

The use of USAID reports and first hand personnel accounts are of large importance in understanding the current status of Afghanistan governance in reference to its links to development in remote areas. In the USAID Interim Report of 2011, Afghan Minister of Education Ghulam Farook Wardak reported "We will increase our focus on the most deprived children, especially girls, in the most remote and least secure parts of our country. Instead of waiting for security to come, we decided to invest more in education as a means to achieving stability" (USAID 2011, 18). As of April 2012, the Afghan National Government and the Paktika Provincial Government were reporting

24

over 20 schools open and being supported financially within the Bermal district; however, coalition forces on site within the district reported zero schools open for business (DAT-Bermal 2012). The discrepancy between the claim of the Afghan Government and the ground truth in this case is an example of how reports from various sources can differ and give an explanation of why some can claim a mission is succeeding while others assess it to be failing.

In 2009 under the support of Admiral Mullen, then-Chairman of the Joint Chiefs of Staff, the Department of Defense initiated the Afghanistan-Pakistan Hands (AFPAK Hands) Program. The premise of the program is to develop a cadre of military and senior civilian experts specializing in the complexities of Afghanistan and Pakistan. Since its inception the program has produced large amounts of information and reports; one continuous report that will be cited through this analysis is the Leader Development Education for Sustained Peace (LDESP). The LDESP provides current status of a variety of Afghanistan issues and of key subjects such as governance and civil society, the economy, and reconstruction and development.

Another major source of information, which is carefully taken into account throughout the analysis, is the media and its publications or interviews directly addressing the current status of the ongoing stabilization of Afghanistan. In a September 2008 Washington Post article "A Modern Taliban Thrives in Afghanistan," Pamela Constable argues that a new reenergized Taliban movement has filled the gap left by the government in a lot of areas by creating parallel government structures largely supported by the dissatisfaction of the Afghan people with President Karzai's government. In February 2011, in an interview for a *New York Times* article "The Next Impasse," Bing

West, former Assistant Secretary of Defense and the author of a book on Afghanistan criticizing the Obama administration's strategy there titled "The Wrong War," explains one of his basic arguments: "American Soldiers and Marines are very good at counterinsurgency, and they are breaking their hearts, and losing their lives, doing it so hard. But the central premise of counterinsurgency doctrine holds that if the Americans sacrifice on behalf of the Afghan government, then the Afghan people will risk their lives for the same government in return. This is not happening" (Filkins 2011).

In an effort to understand West's view regarding the lack of ownership from the Afghan people, but in no way to justify it, the analysis takes into account ideas and thoughts from Pakistani journalist and author Imtiaz Gul. Mr. Gul alludes to the fact that the people of Afghanistan are willing to support, if not tolerate, the shadow governments of Islamist movements, to provide at a minimum a sense of fairness, justice and equal citizenship that comes with accepting this unofficial government and sharia law (Gul, 2009, 53). Gul's *The Most Dangerous Place: Pakistan's Lawless Frontier*, explores the modern history of the Afghanistan/Pakistan border with an emphasis on the North and South Waziristan regions of the FATA. The tribal dynamics and complexities in the region, as explained in Gul's research, provide a critical view and background of the reluctance of Waziristan leaders and residents as they are asked to support a federal government from which they receive few, if any, benefits. The text also renders the association and influence of known Taliban leaders, sub-organizations, and supporters in the Waziristan region combating any legitimacy and efforts of the local government.

The attacks on the legitimacy of the local government, not only in Eastern Paktika and Waziristan but in many other regions of Afghanistan, also come in the form of the

26

campaign of insurgent leaders to gain the support of these areas' populations. In a 22 December 2009 unclassified brief by U.S. Army Major General Michael Flynn (ISAF Director of Intelligence) points out Mullah Omar's (Taliban Leader) guidance for his population-centric strategy. Mullah Omar's message to his subordinates was simple, "This is our mission: to keep people and their property safe. Do not let those people that love money take our local people's property and cause them problems. Keep good relationships with your friends and the local people, and do not let the enemy divide/separate you" (Flynn 2009). Mullah Omar's understanding of the conflict's COG (the population) is obvious, which because of his presence in regions like Eastern Paktika and the absence of the Afghan Government provides his elements an advantage that drives at the heart of the problem.

Over the period of twelve months the author, in direct collaboration with many of the sources previously mentioned DoS, USAID, PRT, SFA Teams, Coalition Forces along with Special Operation Forces gathered and reported local government status, issues and shortfalls to provincial- and national-level Afghan and ISAF leaders and organizations in an effort to assist in the development of a way ahead for the Bermal District of Eastern Paktika and many of the surrounding areas. These daily reports and area overviews cover an array of aspects that weighed heavily and in many ways continue to do so with regard to the legitimacy and effectiveness of the Bermal local government. These firsthand accounts and primary sources information are the difference between what is being reported at the provincial- and national-level and the ground truth.

CHAPTER 3

RESEARCH METHODOLOGY

Drop by drop a river is formed.

— Afghan proverb

The purpose of this analysis is not only to assess the progress that is being reported in the Eastern region of the Paktika Province in Afghanistan and the challenges the area faces, but also to identify more clearly, and explain the reasons for the differences between the Government of Afghanistan and ISAF end state and the current status of the region. In order to develop a better understanding of the role of governance and how it facilitates stability in the context of counterinsurgency, the author will reference several historical case studies during the analysis, with the current situation in the Eastern Paktika districts as a contemporary example. The cases are compared in reference to the efforts to stabilize government entities at different stages and points in time, to determine their effectiveness.

Case Study Criteria

When considering one of the main objectives of counterinsurgency, gaining or maintaining the support of the local population, the idea of "local, fair and legitimate government" is closely associated. To conclude whether government stability and effectiveness in the specific region of Eastern Afghanistan is progressing or faltering, the analysis must be based on clear criteria which support a pre-defined end state. Due to the abstract nature of political issues within the realm of governance, the criteria can be qualitative or quantitative. For the purpose of this study the criteria chosen to deal with this complex topic are a group of basic evaluation concepts or objectives. The themes or parameters used to determine levels of success are: (1) Identify and recruit local leaders and organizational representatives, (2) Reestablish (or establish for the first time) the justice system (law enforcement and legal courts), (3) Reestablish (or establish for the first time) essential services provided by local government, to include educational and medical capacity, and (4) Secure the populace continuously (Department of the Army 2006, 156). These parameters are critical for the development of a local government and therefore are an inherent part of the analysis.

With these chosen criteria, the study makes several comparisons using examples based on the British operations in Waziristan (border region of East Afghanistan and Western Pakistan; FATA) during the 1930s. The British efforts during this period revolved around the competing systems of "Sandeman System" and "Close Border System" as to how to deal with the frontier tribes of the North West of India (region which after 1947 became Pakistan) (Bruce 1938, 3; Gul 2012, 1). These systems were the British attempt at stabilizing the region's tribal government in the form of law, order and control. The study also references events and data from comparisons made of the efforts of the US and the use of the CORDS program to engage the population, gain their support, and defeat an insurgency during the Vietnam conflict.

Effective Governance Analysis Methodology

The methodology to analyze the case studies used is a comparison of the similar scenarios, regions, and strategies intended to help stabilize, and promote an effective governance mechanism. The study further examines the results of these strategies and programs to account for their possible success, their failures, their challenges and the eventual long-term consequences they create in their respective time frames and future developments in the region. Focusing on the "build" phase of the "clear-hold-build" approach to counterinsurgency the analysis draws evaluation methods by associating themes within the build phase. Government support and development of governance capacities assist this building theme, which include protecting the population, and providing an overall benefit to the community (Department of the Army 2007, 5-68).

The comparison then focuses on the assessment portion of the results based on the criteria with two types of assessment measures: MOPs and how these measures subsequently support the outcome that is being sought after, the MOEs. MOPs are used to assess friendly action tied in to a specific task and its accomplishment. MOEs are used to assess the achieving of an objective, the creation of an effect, or to assess the changes in a system behavior (Department of the Army 2007, 5-94). A simple example staying within the stability theme is: the desire to improve education and literacy levels in the rural areas of Afghanistan can be used as a desired effect. The MOPs in this case could be the number of schools that have been built in a specific region, with the MOEs being the increase in literacy rates in the same region associated with those schools. The table below is an example table of the format that is used later in the analysis to reflect the criteria, the MOPs, the MOEs and the result based for these efforts.

Table 1.	MOP/MOE Example Table		
Desired Effect (Criteria)	**MOP**	**MOE**	**Effect Attained Y/N: Why?**
Improve education and literacy levels in the rural areas.	Build Schools in the target area.	Increase from 20% to 60% of all kids in the region attending school.	Y: Increased attendance to local schools.

Source: Created by author.

Methodological Limitations

Assessing the effectiveness of governance just like other conceptual themes such as leadership is inherently difficult. However, when the tools to assess that effectiveness are clearly defined, the parameters well chosen and the cases to be assessed well illustrated, this difficult process can be attempted, although it will always be subject to interpretation. One of the major limitations of the study is using data, reports and firsthand accounts from several sources which in many cases have similar but not completely equal objectives, resulting in opposing ideas and suggestions on the same issues. The other limitation is the immense amount of data in general that is currently available, which would require an additional study and time to gather, allocate as quantitative or qualitative, and then analyze.

Contemporary Case Study Data Collection

The case study chosen was selected because of the availability of primary sources to include the author. While a substantial portion of the data collected is general and open to the public, most of the on-the-ground verification or disagreement was done through personal interviews. These interviews were conducted with key personnel in various positions within the stability operations circles in the Paktika Province and its Eastern region. Using electronic correspondence, telephone conversations and a list of predetermined questions to guide the interview, the author uses the information gained to first describe the connection and relation of the personnel being interviewed to the region, their experiences with the subject being analyzed and to confirm or deny reports introduced in this analysis. To maintain the integrity of the study, all interviewees were provided informed consent to have their interview used as part of the thesis and subsequent publication. The interviews are listed in Appendix B, with the actual questions and answers available upon request. While most of the data available on this subject can be obtained and managed through open sources, some material is still classified due to the ongoing operations in Afghanistan and is not available; no classified material was introduced in this analysis.

Summary

The methodology explained in this chapter detailed the analysis of four primary criteria and how they are implemented in each of the case studies. These criteria: (1) Identify and recruit local leaders and organizational representatives, (2) Reestablish justice system, (3) Reestablish essential services provided by local government, including educational and medical capacity, and (4) Secure the populace continuously, are critical elements of a stability effort as applied by the LLOs. The chapter also explains the use of measures of performance versus measures of effectiveness to assess the progress being reported within these criteria.

CHAPTER 4

ANALYSIS

We are content with discord; we are content with alarms; we are content
with blood . . . we will never be content with a master.
— British Commander Mountstuart Elphinstone (from a Waziri tribesman)

An additional aim of this analysis is to identify the importance of the Bermal

district and the Waziristan region. The problems manifesting themselves in Bermal are

some of the same major difficulties that government officials face as they try to secure

public support in this and other rural and unstable areas through Afghanistan. Analyzing

this local district government in the Eastern region of the Paktika Province serves this

aim. It also provides a current example of methodology and strategy to implement a

mechanism for the development of effective governance in some of the most rural,

remote and dangerous areas of Afghanistan. This chapter uses the criteria selected for the

analysis and evaluation of the effectiveness of local governance. While the historical and

contemporary case study comparison of strategies and techniques used are an important

aspect of the analysis, the major result sought is the evaluation and comparison of the

MOPs in direct contrast to the MOEs. In simple terms, what actions were (for the

historical examples) or are being executed to reach the end state, an effective local

government. This in turn must then be compared to the actual effects being created, seen

at the focal points of the problem, the relationship between the population and the

government.

Waziristan

As the evaluation of progress with regards to governance in the region of interest for this analysis is developed, the influence of Waziristan and its tribal dynamics is a critical and essential aspect that must be included. Throughout the rest of the analysis, the author references materials concerning Waziristan, the Waziri Tribe and the sub-tribes and clans within that society. The general and sometimes pointed references further assist in understanding the reasoning behind the historical policies implemented in this area and the ideology used to execute and evaluate governance. To understand the assortment of challenges and complex themes of the Bermal District and surrounding areas, the analysis must visit the development of this region over the last 150 years.

Since the 1849 annexation of the Punjab by the British Empire, one of the biggest challenges that the British faced was how to govern, or even control the North-Western Frontier of India (NWFI), especially Waziristan. The North-Western Frontier of India is divided into the North-West Frontier Province (NWFP) to the North, and Baluchistan to the South. This strip of tribal territory makes up the mountainous, arduous, and unforgiving border between the North-Western Frontier of India (modern day Pakistan) and Afghanistan. Waziristan extends to the southernmost portion of the NWFP from its northern boundaries, bordering Baluchistan to the North (Bruce 1938, 1). Due to Waziristan's reputation as a lawless region and people, along with the inability of the British (Indian) or Afghanistan governments to control the region with any success, the region was left to a policy of nonintervention by all (Watteville 1925, 6).

In November 1893, as part of an agreement between Sir Mortimer Durand (representing the British Empire) and Afghan Amir Abdur Rahman Khan, the demarcations for a border between Afghanistan and India were made and subsequently referred to as "the Durand Line." This agreement placed most of Waziristan under Indian sovereignty. However, the Durand Line failed to recognize ethnographical and topographical factors. The agreement and institution of new barriers between Afghanistan and India served to divide the Waziristan area into two parts. Similar to the Berlin wall separating the German people, the Durand Line separated the Waziri tribes. This agreement, as explained by writer Sir Martin Ewans, is only magnified by the division of tribes and in many occasions' villages themselves. With a continuing policy of nonintervention by either government, the tribesman viewed this border as a challenge to their independence and essentially ignored it (Roe 2010, 84-86).

As depicted in figure 4, this border created a major challenge for the residents of the Bermal District of Afghanistan. While Bermal has small elements of Kharoti Pashtuns tribe members along its borders with the other districts of the Paktika province, over 90 percent of its residents are Waziri Pashtuns of the Utmanzai and Ahmadzai sub-tribes of which the majority is in Pakistani territory (NPS 2011). The separation of elements of the Utmanzai and Ahmadzai sub-tribes from the main body of the tribe in Pakistan might appear insignificant in the larger picture of the Islamic Republic of Afghanistan. However, this ignored and uninformed division created by the Durand line, in addition to the nonintervention policy, possibly accounts for the lack of support for the Afghan Government by the Bermal residents, as their allegiance defaults to their tribesmen due to both affiliation (family) and proximity. As a reflection of their tribal hierarchy and traditions, allegiance is primarily given to the family, then the tribe, then the ethnic group and finally their country. The map reflects Bermal is the only part of Waziristan on the Afghan side of the Durand Line (Roe 2010, 164).

A surprising example of the modern state of mind of many Bermal residents was observed by coalition forces in 2011. An older villager entered the district center requesting to see the District Governor (DGOV) Hajji Zaher. Because of the manner of appointing district governors by the Afghan Government (which the analysis will address), the DGOV did not know this villager. The villager stated his business, "I need a letter (a letter of reference) from the governor identifying me as a good villager." The DGOV agreed to write the letter and asked some pertinent questions: name, tribe, where he lives, etc. When asked where he lived, the villager answered by pointing at a village approximately one kilometer from the district center, approximately 10 kilometers from the "Durand Line." When asked why he needed the letter, he responded, "So I can get a Tashkera (official identification card) from the provincial capital Sharana." Finally, when asked why he needed a Tashkera he responded, "Because I want to go to Afghanistan." The inference of the story is that here is a villager, an Afghan that has lived in this region all his life, just as his father did before him and his grandfather before him. They are unaware they are living in Afghanistan, due to the remoteness of their location, their primitive life style, lack of education, and neglect by the Afghan government. While somewhat humorous, the story reflects the typical Waziri and Pashtun ignorance present in the Bermal region and the rural population's sentiment regarding the Afghan government. A small percentage of the population is aware and acknowledges that they are in Afghanistan; the majority consider themselves Waziries or in some cases Pakistanis; therefore creating a very difficult dynamic and an obstacle to political awareness in the area by the Afghan government (DAT-Bermal 2012).

The Analysis

In keeping with the methodology the subsequent historical case studies, starting with the British experiences and challenges during early 1900s as they dealt with the NWFP of India and with the Waziristan region specifically; following with the efforts for pacification of the government of South Vietnam in the 1950s and 1960s; and finishing with the analysis of the current status of ISAF's efforts in Afghanistan. All three cases are focus on the governance LLO using the preselected criteria of: (1) Identifying and recruit local leaders and organizational representatives, (2) Reestablishing the justice system, (3) Reestablishing essential services, and (4) Secure the populace continuously (Department of the Army 2006, 156).

The selection of only four criteria, which are equivalent to the general objective and tasks within the LLO, was deliberate as to attempt to evaluate all criteria (objectives) delineated within this theme would exceed the parameters of time available and would require an additional and broader analysis.

The British in Waziristan

Identifying the True Leaders

While the British approach to govern and control the Baluchistan region of the NWFI by using the "Sandeman System" was very successful, the opposite was true for their approach to the NWFP to the North. The approach of a "Close Border System," which has been addressed previously also as the system of nonintervention, failed primarily because it veered away from the supreme test of "the welfare of the tribes," upon which the Sandeman System was based (Bruce 1938, 3). The selection of this Close Border System is an important aspect of the directly linked to the identifying and recruiting local leaders and representatives to administer the volatile areas in the NWFP. The success of the Sandeman System was largely due to the efforts of Sir Colonel Robert Sandeman around 1866. His emphasis on peace and goodwill proved welcome, as he pushed forward with the betterment of the Balochistan region which benefitted the British and Indian governments by establishing security of the Quetta trade route. The success of governmental influence in Balochistan is said to also be a result of the much calmer and less volatile demeanor of the Baloch, which facilitated the interaction between the government and the tribes. This interaction and ability to work with the Waziri tribes was lacking when compared to the Pashtuns of Northern Waziristan (Heeg 2011, 8).

With intervention deemed impractical in areas such as Waziristan, the British forces left the Waziri tribes alone, thereby allowing them to continue following their tribal systems of governance. The local tribal and religious leaders, along with the local *Jirga* continued to be the primary actors of their governance, emphasizing the obedience to their cultural and religious laws and customs. In the 1890s R. I. Bruce, then Commissioner of *Darajat,* in an attempt to further assist and support *The Malik System* which he had instituted in Waziristan attempted to introduce the successful Sandeman System within this region (Roe 2010, 87). In similar fashion to the Malik System the Sandeman system exercises governmental control through the tribal leaders and their traditional systems. This allows the government to have a mechanism and representatives within the tribes that it could pressure to influence actions on other members of the tribe. One of the major problems with this attempt at mimicking the Sandeman System was that Bruce had selected the *Maliks* to represent the tribes and did not allow the tribes to select the Maliks themselves. This provided a major gap, leaving out of the view and knowledge of the British Government key leader not identified. Commissioner Bruce acted independently without considering the effects of his actions. In selecting the Maliks, he had unwittingly isolated a number of influential tribesmen and other influential individuals who could have been engaged and empowered to assist the government in the region (Roe 2010, 88). Ultimately, Commissioner Bruce's attempts to work with the tribes proved ineffective and resulted in a greater reluctance on the part of the Waziri to identify with the established government.

The poor performance of Bruce's attempt was that intervention and continued presence by the British in this region was non-existent, creating poor to no oversight by the government over these *Maliks* and other representatives. During this period the Indian (British) answer to oversight and governance was the "British Political Officer". The political officer (PO) was at the heart of this era of nonintervention; their role was more of exercising personal influence rather than authority as they dealt with the tribal leadership and their concerns. They were charged with being the intermediaries of the Indian and British Governments to navigate the intricacies of tribal culture and politics (Roe 2010, 212).

However, due to the inherent danger of the political officer's position, duties, and location, they were discouraged and at times forbidden to cross the boundaries into the areas of nonintervention. This restriction created a dependency on the use of "middlemen" (or go-betweens) to maintain visibility in their assigned areas. To the detriment of the relationship between the tribes and the government, many of these middlemen succumbed to the allures of corruption, power and wealth (Bruce 1938, 3). With minimal presence in the "protected areas," as these nonintervention areas were being also called, the British were only venturing into the region when expeditions were necessary to curtail problems or address critical issues. During the late 1890s, expeditions into the region became more and more frequent under the direction of Lord Curzon. Curzon's push to update the frontier policy to a "control from within" strategy, (Bruce 1938, 4) only reformed the military aspect of British presence in the North-West Frontier Province, which he established in November 1901. However these attempts to involve themselves in Waziristan would fall short with the British settling for the safeguarding of areas that they already controlled, including Wana, Tochi and Kurram Valleys (Roe 2010, 92).

Exploring new methods of curtailing conflicts and exercising some sort of control

over the area, but willing to settle for containment, the British Empire resorted to the use

of incentives, and payment of allowances to the tribes. While in contemporary use this

might be considered absurd, the "pay off" of the tribes to monitor and control themselves,

it can be argued a more cost-effective method of security; producing instant results,

ensuring that the tribal problems and disputes stay within the confines of their areas and

do not spill over and affect the other regions (Roe 2010, 239). With all its complexity, the

outcome for all British attempts at controlling and assisting the government in this region

kept fomenting the same nonintervention policy. leaving the *Maliks* and religious leaders

governing the people; which continued to be an issue due to these leaders having

credibility and legitimacy issues for been selected by Britain.

Reestablishing Justice

During the early 1900s, as a result of the continuation of the British policy of

nonintervention, the Indian Penal Code and court system that was to be executed in the

tribal territory was ignored by the tribes. The disregard for this code and system left the

primary source of legal and rule of law mechanisms to the PO assigned to the region and

their assistants (Roe 2010, 107). Their duties in regards to the justice system in the area

were: to discourage tribes from raiding, arrest offenders and outlaws, round up raiding

gangs and settle tribal disputes. However, the PO's efficiency and effectiveness was

limited in large part by their hands-off approach to the tribal territories. Even the

Assistant Political Officers (APO) that were chosen for their Pashtun heritage and

knowledge were out of place when transplanted into the Waziri culture. The traditional

court system and normal Indian law only extended to government property (army

42

cantonments and scout's posts), principal lines of communication, and 100 yards either side of them, with no effort or ability to enforce law and order beyond those boundaries (Roe 2010, 107).

With a political officer system lacking validity and presence, the 6,000 year old tribal systems remained the standard for justice in the region. Considered a *Nang* (honor) tribe, the Waziri emphatically follow their moral honor code known as *Pashtunwali*. However, this code is not limited to the individual Pashtun or Waziri; it has been incorporated into every aspect of tribal society. The code and its interpretation are used for the making of business decisions, social justice, self-determination, equality, cooperation and tolerance (Roe 2010, 42). The power of *Pashtunwali* and its application can be said to usurp Islamic Sharia Law, but has greater roots in Pashtun culture. As explained by Wali Khan (Pakistan's National Awami Party Leader and Pashtun) in 1975 when asked if he was a Muslim, a Pakistani, or Pashtun first? "I am a six-thousand year-old Pashtun, a thousand-year-old Muslim, and a twenty-seven year old Pakistani," he said.

With no other system of law, the Pashtun way and the *Jirga* system of making decisions and settling disputes continued as the primary method of rule of law in the Waziri regions. The British Empire had no ability to impose law and order, so they did nothing. The PO simply monitored and reported on events. Case in point, a notorious Mahsud rebel, Bahram Khan, was arrested, presented to the *Jirga*, and consequently convicted, which carried a level of dishonor (a great shame in Pashtun culture) and had his house destroyed. While the outcome could seem uncivilized and crude, an internal tribal solution without exception was seen as the only alternative (Roe 2010, 48).

43

Reestablish Essential Services

"The welfare of the tribes" was the priority of the British efforts in the NWFP as it had proven successful in Baluchistan utilizing the Sandeman system. From 1923 until the 1947 independence of the region from British control, the British Empire attempted to set forth a more "forward policy". This policy consisted of an increased presence in Waziristan, as well as reforming the Waziristan militias to support the military outposts in Razmak in North Waziristan (primarily inhabited by Utmanzai Waziri) and Wana in South Waziristan. The increased presence did manage to curtail some of the lawlessness amongst the border tribes; however, it was more of a preventive measure rather than a curative one. With some improvements to security, the government was now able to engage the populace, which in time brought the building of primary schools and Western-style health care to the area (Roe 2010, 96).

While the initiative and the intention to deliver these much needed services was a great step, the efficiency and overall support fell short. Mr. F. G. Pratt, then Commissioner of Northern Division in the Province of Bombay, noted a hospital in Miran Shah that was equipped with 16 beds, had an additional 40-50 patients clinging to life in adjacent stables, and thus was unable to meet the demand for health services (Roe 2010, 96). There was no doubt that health facilities and care were needed, as the tribesmen made extensive use of the limited medical facilities throughout Waziristan. For example, in 1923 medical services in North Waziristan were provided to approximately 8,000 patients. By 1932, the number had escalated to 133,000 tribesmen and their families. While some cultural norms such as *Purdah* (gender separation) were still impeding the process of providing health care, the tribes continued to accept the Western-

44

style medicine and worked compromises for the treatment of the community (Roe 2010, 205).

Unfortunately, the British failed to capitalize on this golden opportunity to influence the "middle ground" of the community and gain their trust. The legitimacy of the government also started to fade, primarily due to the limitation of resources and, arguably, due to the inability or unwillingness of the government to maximize the support for the medical efforts in these tribal areas. An effort that at its onset could have created a long lasting effect in a known inhospitable region fell short because of the inability of the government authorities to continue to provide such resources. For example, in 1937, the government had 10,000 horses and 800 camels with its accompanying veterinarians and medications. While their use might have been limited, these types of elements which were attached to infantry and scout units could have alleviated some of the problems extending from the need of veterinary services through the region. However, the authorities were reluctant to commit to what they saw could become a long term strategy and never ending commitment (Roe 2010, 207).

This reluctance to invest in a long term strategy was also being transmitted through the education system or lack thereof. The frontier schools that accompanied the forward policy, just as the health care facilities, were overcrowded and underfunded. An even more concerning second order effect, as Sir William Barton explained (British Parliamentarian: 1906-1909), was that young tribesmen with an education had to be given appointments to legitimate positions, or risk becoming prey to political agitators from British India. With the reality of no available appointments, the efforts of the government to encourage development into the tribal areas were seen as a danger, whose only objective was to change the culture (Roe 2010, 198).

The challenges and failures of the push for essential services in Waziristan by the British came as a result of the continuous rejection by the tribesmen, for the trust and viewed as interference in their customs and beliefs with minimal or zero benefit to the community. The government was finally recognizing that this intervention would continue to create resentment and hostility, and once again return to their policy of nonintervention.

Securing the Populace

Securing the North-West Frontier Province, especially the Waziristan region, has eluded local, foreign forces and governments for centuries. The British did not have the resources to control the area, so they adopted their policy of nonintervention. Governing by proxy seemed to be an appropriate term when speaking of the NWFP or as Sir Olaf Caroe, Governor of NWFP 1946-1947, said "In other words, it was the principle of indirect rule." Using the *Maliks* as the intermediary, the British physical control of the region was minimal. For the most part it was a state of anarchy and lawlessness, which did no more than pay lip service to the *Maliks*, saving their attentiveness for the *Fakirs* (holy man/men) in the area (Roe 2010, 48).

With the British resigned to let the regions govern themselves, the concept of recruiting and using *Kassadar* (local tribal policemen) also known as scouts or the *Irregular Frontier Corps* (made up of indigenous members) became prevalent, to have a law enforcement body or military presence in the regions (Roe 2011). Reaching in excess of 5,400 by 1935, *Kassadar* were frequently tasked by the government to perform an array of security requirements, but their role remained as servants of the tribe. They were a security force, paid by the government, consisting of indigenous members, who remained in their own territory while performing these tasks.

The use of *Kassadar* was viewed positively by the British Government, especially in the mid-1930s as trouble erupted in the region; however, there was a high degree of distrust and animosity from the Indian army towards the *Kassadars*. The cultural, ethnic, and custom differences made it difficult for *Kassadar* to be trusted in the eyes of the regular Indian military, which were the main organized force in the region. The distrust made mutual support difficult as the Indian/British forces would ask for the withdrawal of *Kassadar* elements from areas where official military operations were to be conducted. This distrust, along with continuous issues with pay delays and *Kassadars* being passed over for promotion consistently deteriorated the relationship and the reliability on the *Kassadar* elements. The result of many of these issues in some cases would be disbanding, suspension and punishing of entire company *Kassadar* size elements, by the government. This nullified any positive gains the presence of the indigenous elements had made within the region (Roe 2010, 114).

Due to the problems dealing with the *Kassadars*, a midlevel supervising entity was used to coordinate and attempt at facilitating the relationship between them and the Indian Army. The Frontier Scouts filled in this role somehow effectively, while performing their primary roles of private militia for the political agents of the region. While the scouts were also tribesmen from the region, their focus and their guidance came directly from the British officers appointed within their ranks, the political officers, and obviously the Indian (British) Government (Roe 2010, 120). The use of Kassadar units contributed greatly to the self-governance and securing of the region, however it was not without its problems. Absenteeism (primarily due to inherent different way of life), lack of training, and the selection process resulted their neglect and abuse by the government, feeding further the discontent from the tribes to the government (Roe 2010, 115). "There is no hope of weaning the tribesmen from their wild independence; therefore, the best policy to adopt is to leave him to stew in his own juice in the hills" (Sir William Barton).

Table 2. British Results in Waziristan			
Desired Effect (Criteria)	MOP	MOE	Effect Attained Y/N: Why?
Identifying the True Leaders	Use of PO and the Malik system.	Reduction of incursions into Waziristan, and increase of tribal autonomy.	N: British/Indian government had minimal control or say in Waziristan region.
Reestablishing Justice	Allow the tribal system to conduct all legal actions.	Increase of tribal autonomy.	N: British/Indian government unable to enforce penal/legal codes.
Reestablish Essential Services	Building of schools and clinics in tribal region.	1923-1932, increase in tribesmen getting health care (8,000 to133,00).	Y: British/Indian government assumed a forward intervention policy.
Securing the Populace	Introduction of tribal lead security efforts (Kassadars).	By 1935 Kassadar elements increased to 5,400.	N: British/Indian government had no control or trust for Kassadar elements.

Source: Created by author.

As reflected in the above table the British government struggled with this region and its efforts for several decades more until the conception of the Islamic Republic of

Pakistan in 1930, and its consequent independence in 1947 from the British Empire. They continued to encounter conflicts to pacify as they attempted to maintain control of their colonies, as it was the case from 1948 to 1957 during the Malaya emergency. Counterinsurgency lessons learned during this period eventually made their way to the British advisory mission, where they in conjunction with the US assisted pacification efforts in support of Vietnam's president Diem during the 1950s. As American involvement escalated in the 1960s, it appeared that the counterinsurgency torch had been passed to the US efforts from the British Empire.

Vietnam 1950s and 1960s

Identifying the True Leaders

Prior to its colonial period under the French, Vietnam was the embodiment of centralized monarchy. This monarchy established a fixed hierarchy with a rank structure that selected and appointed all public officials (Mandarins) to all levels of political and military positions. While the positions were filled and assigned through a civil service examination, the recipients, as a rule, were wealthy society members. The Mandarins were the dispenser of governance, justice and administration for the emperor throughout the country, down to the provincial and village-level (Britannica 2013).

The eventual arrival of Governor-General Paul Doumer of France was one of the culminating stages of the on-going penetration by France, initiated by Napoleon III in 1857. The impact in the governance arena was immediate, as the French deposed at will of Vietnamese officials and replaced them with personnel from France or individuals loyal to the French. These handpicked Vietnamese officials benefitted immensely from the labor of the peasant population, which was deprived of the most basic of benefits

49

(Britannica 2013). While villages and provinces still followed their tribal and family structures, any decisions of importance to their economical or political advancement were made outside of their circles.

The exit of French forces from South Vietnam in 1954, as a result of the Geneva Accords, created a void that the Vietnamese were not prepared to fill. Consequently this further destabilized the governance mechanism which would affect the pacification efforts of the government and its Western associates in the future. The once traditional village level autonomous governments that raised revenue, drafted budgets, and exercised responsible adjudication of their laws, were disadvantaged by the French opposition to their self-rule since their arrival in Indo-China. Due to the heavy control of local elections and councils, along with all the restrictions imposed by the French, the Vietnamese government was now unprepared to provide the basic governance framework to its population (Hunt 1995, 10-11).

On 26 June 1954, the Government of South Vietnam (GVN) welcomed from exile their new leader Ngo Dinh Diem. Diem returned with the assistance of the United States Government and its support to lead the efforts to maintain Vietnam as an independent and noncommunist nation (Nagl 2005, 118). However, this was not to be an easy task, because French colonial rule had not prepared the Vietnamese government or the population for independence let alone the way for an effective governance mechanism. The new government was required to offer and provide protection and services to the people as well as defeat a rising insurgency (Hunt 1995, 10).

From his election in 1955 until his assassination in November 1963, President Diem launched an aggressive campaign against the VC shadow government with early success by his secret police the Cong An. While the Cong An received some accolades during this period, they also were linked to allegations of abuse of power throughout South Vietnam. Consequently many members of the Cong An were arrested or forced to flee once the new regime had taken power. Even as the new government of South Vietnam tried to vindicate many of the violations linked to Diem and his forces, his legacy was hard to break as he had handpicked many of this Cong An members, provincial and district chiefs due to their political loyalty or personal connection, rather than their competence. These appointments resulted in the alienation of the communities from the government and created convenient opportunities by the VC shadow government (Moyer 1997, 36). In some instances where local leaders were available to guide within their own original communities, the national leaders avoided assigning these district and provincial leaders to their native regions, which took away any aspect of familiarity, personal or tribal ties to the region. This of course also resulted in added stress to the already alienated population and further separation from central government (Moyer 1997 120).

As United States intervention increased in South Vietnam its efforts to combat the encroachment of the communist North Vietnamese Army and its irregular forces, the inefficiency of the local level governments became more important. With 44 provinces and 234 districts to engage and deal with, a push for a civil-military effort and a more population-centric strategy was needed. In efforts to re-engage the pacification attempts and after the failure of the Office of Civil Operations (OCO) initiative in November 1966, President Johnson implemented Robert Komer's concept of civil-military plans, giving birth to the CORDS program (Andrade 2006). Komer who had served under the

CIA since 1947 and briefly as National Security Advisor, now became President Johnson's primary advisor on pacification in Vietnam.

Leading the effort at the provincial level for the CORDS were usually high ranking Vietnamese Army or Marine officers (Colonels), advised in matters of administration and pacification programs by American provincial advisory teams. These provincial elements and leaders were charged with exercising authority over the district-level governments and their district chiefs in aspects of pacification and rural development. However, the tainted pool of district and provincial level leaders continued to create an obstacle for the efforts of the CORDS program, and to the legitimacy of any GVN efforts through the conflict.

Reestablishing Justice

As a method of neutralizing communist effects in the rural areas of South Vietnam, the GVN allowed and even promoted the arrest Viet Cong Irregulars (VCI) and non-communist civilians, as "an tri" detainees. Different from criminals, these individuals were detained under suspicion of being VCI and VCI supporters, who made up the largest part of the arrests during this period. According to some statistics, for every one hundred arrests only one true VCI or VCI supporter was found (Moyer 2007, 204). However, once the arrest occurred, the process of adjudicating the case had to be initiated.

The adjudication of all cases was presided over by a Provincial Security Committee, composed of the provincial chief and other senior provincial officials, who met once a week, more seldom in some provinces than others. Their primary mission was to oversee the cases of these alleged VCI. As expected, after decades of French rule and its interruption of the pre-existing village and tribal legal mechanisms, the local village (hamlet) rule of law was diminished and relegated to these provincial security committees. Poorly trained, the committees had no guidelines, nor did they have accessibility to lawyers or legal professionals and, were forced to make hasty legal decisions due to the immense number of cases and the short time to process them. While American criticism of the Vietnamese legal system called for improvements and desperately needed reforms of the judicial system, the third world country of Vietnam was far from able to mimic the Western style of rule of law. First because of its deficient training in rule of law, second because of the inherent requirement for educational reforms needed to attempt to run such a system, and finally it would have demanded a fundamental change in Vietnamese culture and in the manner it addresses legal rights and that of defendants (Moyer 2007, 205).

The consequences of such a misguided and uneducated legal system were the arrests of tens of thousands of civilians per year during the 1960s (under the suspicion of being VCI). The CORDS advisors monitored the misuse of the legal system, but did not intervene in any meaningful way. Due to the complexity of the conflict and the constant face off between anti-communist elements and communist North Vietnam the majority of crimes being pursued and legal decisions being made were regarding arrest and convictions of these VCIs and sympathizers. However, due to the same focus on a specific type of crime and criminal, for the most part when an arrest was made the authority and right of adjudication was given to the military channels. With the allied advisors intending to jump start the self reliance of the GVN and empowering it, they chose not interfere into detainee operations and questioning by the GVN officials. This left the GVN to proceed in whatever fashion they wanted, resulting in the torturing and execution of thousands of alleged VCI and their sympathizers (Moyer 2007, 92). The result of the overzealous political influence over the legal system was the arrest of thousands of people, their tortured, and execution for their political affiliation, which further alienated the populace from its government, and contributed to the episodes of grave human rights violations and/or war crimes.

Reestablish Essential Services

Early is his tenure, Ngo Dinh Diem, as the new leader of the South Vietnamese government, pushed forward with his attempt at pacification, as used by the United States and the French government before them. Pacification is defined by the Oxford English Dictionary as "to reduce to peaceful submission, to establish peace and tranquility in a country or district." President Diem's attempt at pacification would prove ineffective after his heavy promises from Diem of supporting rural communities' interest were proven false. Programs executed, such as the one by Kieu Cong Cung, a former Viet Minh commander with the support of General Lansdale (U.S. Advisor to the French in Vietnam in their struggle with the Viet Minh). Cung's program dispatched small teams known as cadre to assist the rural populations with their development, which at the end were unsuccessful.

These cadre (civil servants) along with construction of schools and medical dispensaries, the teachers and health workers to accompany them, to provide the basic services that the communities needed, became the forefront of such programs. The initial failure of this program originated with the teams of cadre, who on many occasions took these assignments to be a punishment, as the majority had original assignments in Saigon,

54

and now had to endure primitive living, eating and working conditions in the rural regions of Southern Vietnam. Another setback to projects of this nature, was the growing influence of President Diem's brother Ngo Dinh Nhu (Unofficial commander of the ARVN Special Forces and the Cần Lao also known as the Personalist Labor Party), who imposed unwarranted obligations on the rural communities using the cadre teams to impose his will, which overshadowed any positive reviews of the programs (Hunt 1995, 20).

With a new methodology and unbeknownst to the American elements (to include the CORDS mentors) overseeing pacification efforts in South Vietnam, President Diem initiated his controversial "agrovilles" or relocation program, notifying the American advisors after the program was already on its way. The program's focus was to attempt to protect the population by consolidating and relocating entire communities into strong rural compounds. The agrovilles included schools, medical facilities, electricity and other social services within them, which the GVN believed would increase stability and decrease the immense amounts of assassinations, and kidnappings of rural officials that were sent to these regions to work and assist these facilities and government efforts. The program had some merit in trying to secure and protect the community and the assigned government officials. However, problem with the program was that the government continuously overextended its resources when building these compounds. The premise of the program was to use the future residents of the agrovilles to build these fortified communities. But as a result of the lack of resources the agrovilles did not have the capacity to house the promise number of individuals or families (Hunt 1995, 20). This misuse of the labor force created further discontent in the villages towards the government, nullifying the positive influence it was trying to promote.

The agroville program moved forward in 1959, trying to mimic the British efforts in Malaya, but, by 1961, it was a failure due to the poor planning and the decision to expand quickly, overextending the government's capacity to secure and support the agrovilles. However, continuing within the same theme in 1962 the GVN was urged by the US advisors to reinitiate the same program with some adjustments. This new program, known as the "strategic hamlets program," gave a higher priority to the security efforts of the chosen communities (Moyer 1997, 36). Once again, the program met with failure as the GVN continued to overextend its limitations assuming risk in security and its inability to provide support for the hamlets. This allowed the VC to increase attacks on vulnerable locations, driving a larger wedge between the GVN and its population, as they not only affected the security but hindered any efforts to provide the community with the essential services that were part of these hamlets (Pentagon Papers 1971).

As the US ramped up its efforts of pacification in South Vietnam, in conjunction with the increase of security assistance programs specifically the Regional Forces (RF) and the Popular Forces (PF), and carrying out advisory roles, the pacification theme also took form through the involvement of civil affair operations in the critical rural areas of the Vietnam countryside (Hunt 1995, 45). Having minimal success with the OCO, the GVN and American efforts turned to the CORDS program and its six primary subprograms: New Life Development, Chieu Hoi (open arms; a reintegration program for VCI), Revolutionary Development Cadre, Refugee Support, PSYOP, and Public Safety. Under these programs the shift of popular support against the VC and North Vietnamese message continued to grow. Initiatives such as the distribution of farming land, parceling out land to every family in South Vietnam under a new land reform assisted the reenergized support for the GVN. Additional new health care reforms aided in the growth and multiplication of medical facilities and care providers, expanding from 10 dentists, 8 pharmacists and 130 doctors to 74 dentists and 250 pharmacists from 1953 to 1972, and 650 doctors by 1975 (White 2009). The combination and improvement of security and social efforts as a base for these programs started promoting the GVN in a positive manner, gaining popular support in previously difficult areas, and making these efforts produce a success.

Securing the Populace

As World War II came to an end along with the Japanese occupation of Vietnam, the French occupation pushed forward attempting to control and prevent Vietnam from being corrupted by the communist ideology and the influence of China. Their struggle in Vietnam, attempted to eliminate the threat of communism being pushed by North Vietnam, was bloody and unsuccessful, forcing the United States to take a more active role after the final withdrawal of French forces in 1954 (Hunt 1995, 4). Part of this involvement was the US support for Ngo Dinh Diem, as the new leader of Vietnam. Aware of the critical of the security efforts required for the pacification of South Vietnam, President Diem initiated the relocation of communities to agrovilles and eventually to strategic hamlets. This was an attempt to isolate the population away from the VC and North Vietnam influence (Hunt 1995, 22).

Patterned after the "new villages" concept used by the British military during the Malaya Emergency in the late 1940s (Nagl 2002, 74), the GVN pushed forward with the construction of similar fortifications to cut off the insurgent access to the communities. However contrary to the advice of Sir Robert Thompson (British Advisor to Vietnam), President Diem did not use government security forces (police and paramilitary forces) to protect the strategic hamlets. Diem's intention was that the fortifications would be the primary means of protection, with the tying in of the people being defended into that protection plan. Dangerously concerned with quantity of strategic hamlets being constructed and completed, the GVN veered off away from their intended measure of effectiveness, the view towards the government from the population and the balance of political power in such regions. Unable to lessen the influence of the VC in the majority of these hamlets, possibly due to the lack of training and support for the security forces made up by the villagers themselves, and possibly their unwillingness to put themselves in between the insurgency and the government's line of fire, the program came to an end in 1964 (Hunt 1995, 22-25).

While the conventional security forces were still developing and growing into their roles, the progress was being made through unconventional programs as the CIA's Civilian Irregular Defense Group (CIDG). Originating in 1961, the program focused on empowering the villagers by arming them, and providing not only tactical training, but also developmental support under the umbrella and supervision of United States Army Special Forces elements. By 1962, this experiment had, according to the GVN, officially secured/pacified 40 villages in the test province of Buon Enao. Unfortunately, the conventional mind set of the United States continued to control the up-tempo and the types of operations security efforts followed. Leaning towards a more offensive and conventional warfare for the theater, the program was gutted, and the Special Forces mission was redefined to border surveillance and control (Nagl 2005, 128).

After the assassination of President Diem and the coup installing General Nguyen Khanh as the new South Vietnam government leader, the government faced a continual decline of popular support. For the next few years, the proposed revised pacification plan, called Chien Thang (Will to Victory) would fluctuate up and down as to the level of popular support, increments of Regional Forces (RF), Popular Forces (PF) and Police Field Forces (PFF) played a big part in that constant changing support, in many occasions created additional problems due to the lack of supervision from the central powers. But for the most part providing a robust presence and needed security to the populace. By late 1966, the South Vietnam Government had approximately 644,000 security force members. Unable to match the security forces protecting the rural areas of South Vietnam, the VC was forced to resort to terrorist type attacks (Hunt 1995, 43).

American participation and assistance continued until 1973, leaving the security and defense of the Republic of South Vietnam in the hands of its military, which eventually fell to the North Vietnamese attacks in April 1975. This allowed the US military to once again store its counterinsurgency doctrine and focus on the raise of a nuclear threat arising within the Soviet Union and therefore the beginning of the "Cold War."

Table 3.	GVN Program Results in Vietnam		
Desired Effect (Criteria)	**MOP**	**MOE**	**Effect Attained Y/N: Why?**
Identifying the True Leaders	Introduction of Cadre program, District-level leaders selected at National level.	The number of government representatives assigned per hamlet, district or province.	N: Outsiders not chosen by the community, corruption and presence of VC shadow government.
Reestablishing Justice	Establishment of the Provincial Security Committees.	Increase of arrests and adjudication of cases.	N: Corruption, and political persecution, no legal guidelines.
Reestablish Essential Services	Establishment of land and health care reforms.	Increase of medical and dental providers.	Y: Continuous presence of service providers in rural regions.
Securing the Populace	Initiation of "Strategic Hamlet" program, and the establishment of RF and PF security elements.	By 1966 the GVN counted with 644,000 security forces.	Y: Continuous presence in rural contested regions.

Source: Created by author.

The conflict that this rivalry created came to a critical point as in 1978 the People's Democratic Party of Afghanistan (PDPA) with the support of the Soviet Union takes control of the government of Afghanistan, consequently leading to the 19 December 1979 invasion of Soviet troops of Afghanistan in efforts to curtail the remaining opposition to the new government (Coll 2004, 50). In response Afghan freedom fighters operating out of the NWFP, with assistance from the United States fight the Soviet invaders until February 1989, when the last Soviet troops leave Afghanistan. In the aftermath of the Soviet withdrawal Afghanistan without the dynasty and consistency that a monarchy prior to the invasion had once had, dissolved into a violent checkerboard of lawless regions (Coll 2004, 282). In 1994, in an attempt to bring control and order to the country Mullah Mohammad Omar leads the raise of the Taliban, and perceived as popular revolution as he brings an end to the Afghan warlords' control of the country (Coll 2004, 283). On 17 September 2001, after the 11 September attacks on US soil, President Bush signed orders authorizing the CIA to conduct war in Afghanistan (Rashid 2008, 62), consequently leading to the dislodging of Taliban rule of the country.

ISAF in Afghanistan

Identifying the True Leaders

In early April 2011, Hajji Mohammad Zaher arrived as the newly appointed district governor of the Bermal district in Eastern Paktika Province. A veteran public servant, he was assigned by the Provincial Governor Samim, who can appoint temporary district governors with permanent appointment authority resting with President Karzai. Hajji Zaher was completely new to the Bermal district, a member of the Suleimankhel tribe from Southern Paktika and with no ties to the Utmanzai-Waziri who control Bermal, other than both being Pashtun. Zaher's arrival was forced by the replacement of district governor Dawlat Khan (from Wardak tribe) whose transfer to the Kushamond district from Bermal came as the result of his constant disputes and on-going friction with the Waziri tribal leaders in Bermal (DAT-Bermal,2012).

While the Utmanzai and Ahmadzai Waziries displayed a level of respect for Hajji Zaher as the district governor, he had no influence with any of the tribe's leaders and consequently remained an outsider to the community through his tenure in Bermal. Due to his ignorance of the key figures and power brokers in the area, along with his lack of influence, Zaher was unable to recognize, let alone coordinate or work with, the majority of the true tribal and regional leaders. From April 2011 until he was "transferred" to the Waza Khwa district in early October 2011, Zaher was the only political representative for the Afghan government in the Bermal district center and in the area. To the Waziri population of this very volatile area, it seemed evident that the government had no intention of assisting them or working with them, as they clearly did not understand the need for a Waziri leader to lead Waziri communities (DAT-Bermal 2012).

In 2008, USAID, in an effort to legitimize the local district government and increase (in many cases initiate) community participation, assisted the GoA to establish the Afghanistan Social Outreach Program (ASOP). This program aimed at strengthening and improving the effectiveness and responsiveness of local governance through a revival of traditional local Shuras, promoting the cooperation and partnership of tribal leaders and representatives with the government (USAID 2011b). Dispatching District Liaison Officers (DLOs) to selected districts, ASOP initiated the recruitment of willing participants for District Community Councils (DCC). As in the case of the Bermal district, this council of 35 members was to gather the concerns and needs of the community and communicate, coordinate and assist the government in meeting those needs. However, with a district governor and a liaison officer unfamiliar with the area and tribes, but with the authority to nominate and select area representatives, the Bermal DCC became a gathering of mid- and low-level tribal spokesmen. Many of these representatives were more preoccupied with their own aggrandizement, ignoring the community's needs. It is only fair to acknowledge that most of the information discussed by the government officials at these Shuras was being passed on to the true leaders of the tribes at a later time by the attendees. Nevertheless, the unwillingness of this true tribal leaders to participate in these Shuras reflected the true status of support for the local and national government by the Bermal tribes (DAT-Bermal 2012).

Conversely, approximately 14 kilometers South of the Bermal district center, the Shkin area, better known as the Shkin District (an unofficial title as it is part of the Bermal district) continues to show progress and get national attention for its success. The reason for Shkin's success and continuous improvement in its development is largely due to the involvement of its community, the Ahmadzai-Waziri, in their local government. However, many other aspects play a role in this successful outcome. For example the ability of the area's law enforcement to protect and secure the community, which leads to a safe environment for development and growth to occur, which cycles back to the willingness of the local residents and leaders to be involved in official local government meetings, events and decisions (DAT-Bermal 2012). It is also critical to note that one of the reasons for substantially more emphasis being placed on the Shkin district is its strategic location. Border Control Point 213 (BCP-213) and the Angoor Ada Bazaar, one of the major thoroughfares of commerce between Pakistan and Afghanistan, just happens to be in Shkin, making this area a high priority for Afghan and Coalition forces to secure and protect (DAT-Bermal 2012). By contrast, the location of the Bermal district center and the areas that make up the rest of the district have become of less concern to the Afghan government and to coalition forces and for the most part left on their own.

According to the Independent Directorate for Local Governance (IDLG), a government agency responsible for coordinating sub-national governance, the Bermal district center is to be manned by an 18 person staff per the *Tashkiel,* which is the

63

structure of positions within a government mechanism or list of jobs approved and budgeted for by the government to be filled and provide a functional entity at various levels. The Bermal district's tashkiel as of December 2012 had 5 of 18 positions filled, including the Education Manager, the Public Health Official, and the Agriculture, Irrigation and Livestock Official; all of whom were seen at the district center on just a couple of occasions, providing no services to the community since their assignment, which in some cases exceeded a year (DAT-Bermal 2012). Their rare public appearances may be explained by the lack of security in the area, as public officials are often the targeted for assassination attempts by insurgents operating in the region. However, that still leaves the question of what, if anything, these public officials are doing for the people they represent. The remaining two *Tashkiel* members assigned to the district were the district governor and the district's police chief. The Paktika Provincial Government, along with key ministries at the national-level, has attempted to fill the remaining vacant tashkiel positions in Bermal. Unfortunately, few qualified individuals are interested in working in one of the most unsecured regions in Afghanistan (DAT-Bermal 2012).

Throughout 2011 the Afghan Government, national as well as at the provincial level, along with IDLG continued to report partial success in initiating mechanisms at the Bermal district level in efforts to improve local tribal support and overall governance of the area by a Government of Afghanistan entity. The MOPs for this evaluation were the efforts to form and the support given to the district-level ASOP Shuras (the district community council). Consequently the MOEs following these actions were the identification of the 35 member Shura members and the vast number of bi-monthly meetings held to discuss district concerns and issues, and the selection and assignment of tashkiel members to fill the required positions at the district level government (DAT-Bermal 2012). These tashkiel members were to start providing the community with much needed basic assistance. The progress reported by this MOE, and actions was premature. The community council was able to meet; however, these meetings were of no consequence and no decisions were made on behalf of the community or the government. These council members lacked authority to make any decision on behalf of the area's population, which made the bi-monthly Shuras a basic meet and greet of some of the local residents for the district governor. Additionally, the Education Manager, the Public Health Official, and the Agriculture, Irrigation and Livestock Official never participated in any meetings, nor planned, prepared or executed any programs or projects for their community (DAT-Bermal, 2012).

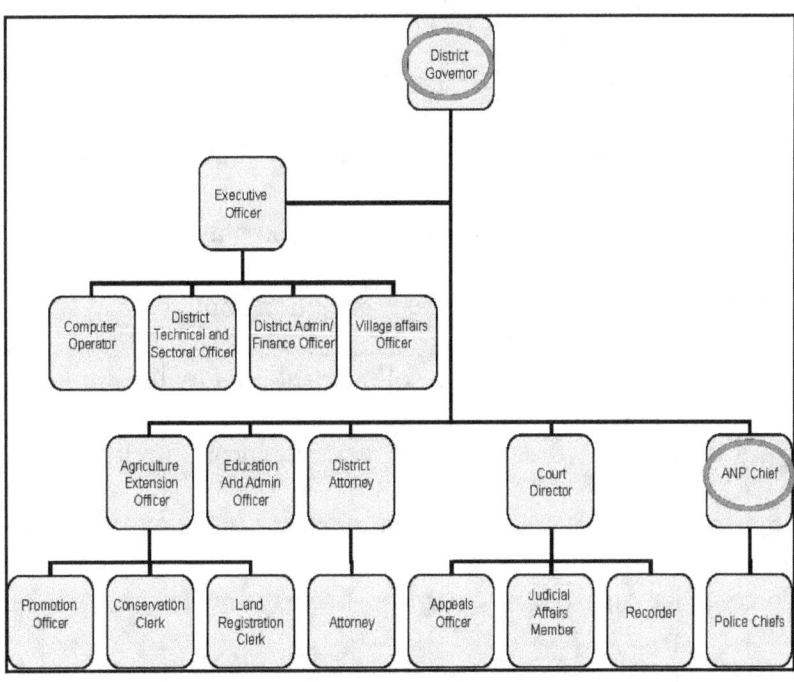

Figure 6.   Afghanistan Model District Diagram

Source: Information Dominance Center (IDC), ISAF Joint Command (IJC), *Model district: 110505*: 5, 22 February 2012.

Encircled in the diagram depicted in figure 6 are the positions the Bermal district actually had on hand (present for duty) to run the district. The diagram also reflects one of many structures the government of Afghanistan has considered and applies to their districts in these rural areas.

Reestablishing Justice

According to the 2010 Sub-National Governance Policy from IDLG and based on the IJC/IDC diagram previously presented in figure 6, a district is authorized and required a District Prosecutor and Judge or equivalent to facilitate and assist in criminal and administrative legal matters. As of December 2012, the Bermal district was still awaiting the assignment of this legal subject matter expert (DAT-Bermal 2012). During the same time frame, the district of Bermal had been forced to follow the interpretation of Afghan law and decrees of the District Police Chief, the District National Directorate of Security Chief and the District Governor. Due to the lack of preparation, training and, in many instances, the absence of law enforcement elements in the region, the Afghanistan National Army (ANA) and its leadership in the area had also played a big role in the interpretation and enforcement of law. While the assumption could be that local law enforcement and military leaders would have a solid grasp of their constitution, laws and regulations, the fact of the matter is that due to the lack of education, illiteracy and absence of paper copies of these documents, the enforcement of rule of law by the Afghan Security Forces is haphazard, uneven, inconsistent, or non-existent. It is, above all, ineffective (DAT-Bermal 2012).

A common case in this high risk area of the Eastern Bermal District is whether or not a private citizen is authorized to own a firearm. The issue becomes more complicated when presented with the knowledge that in Eastern Afghanistan, due to its steady state of conflict through its history, the most common owned weapon is the Kalashnikov AK-47 assault rifle. According to Article 6 of the Afghanistan Official Gazette No 855, under the Afghanistan Criminal Law Penal Code dated 1384 (Lunar Calendar), a person may be authorized to own and maintain a firearm with the proper Ministry of Interior permit. However as the Official Gazette only speaks of sports or hunting firearms and makes no reference to AK-47s (AOG 2011, 25). The problem resulting from this mandate is that with the majority of the Bermal residents are known to own AK-47. ANSF in this case have the legal right to confiscate them, leaving the residents with no self defense alternative in this dangerous region. Adding to the confusion, provincial leaders and previous district leaders had continuously allowed these weapons to be owned by verbal agreements only. While in the legal sense confiscation of these weapons is correct, the effects created in the district and villages are: taking self security out of the hands of the community, with the knowledge that ANSF has not been able to provide that security up to now, and alienating the community from the government by not providing an alternative (residents have asked for exemption to the rule from provincial and national leaders). Problems like these are compounded by the inability of the district government to properly process a case or adjudicate the law. In cases where arrests were made, it became the norm for detainees to remain in a jail cell for days or weeks with no process due to the lack of resources or transportation to a venue with a properly functioning system. With a high level of threat to Afghan National Security Forces (ANSF) in Eastern Afghanistan, vagueness of critical laws and no one to interpret these laws undermines support for the government (DAT-Bermal 2012).

In 2011, a survey by the Asia Foundation reported that in Eastern Afghanistan 81 percent of the population is satisfied with the availability of dispute resolution mechanisms and services in their area (Rennie 2011, 148). Eastern Afghanistan, for the purpose of the report cited, is equivalent to ISAF's Regional Command East which is responsible for operations and the oversight of 14 Afghan provinces to include Paktika. Eastern Afghanistan as it has been defined has a total of 163 districts that when compared to the 6,348 people surveyed of results in approximately 39 people per district that were surveyed. An 81 percent satisfaction rate is a very positive and encouraging number; however, it must also take into consideration the absence of any GoA legal representative at the Bermal district during 2011 and the poor performance by their district governor to adjudicate any disputes (DAT-Bermal 2012). According to the raw data provided by the Asia Foundation no districts information was gathered from the Paktika province in 2011, confirming that the progress reported with the prior percentages did not include the Paktika province or the Bermal district. This information validated even further the perception noted under the same report and using again a base of 6,348 people surveyed, that 92 percent of the respondents agreed that "A Shura/Jirga was available to them" for delivering justice (Rennie 2011 151), as most likely this was the manner in which Bermal continues to practice their rule of law. There is no opposition to disputes being resolved through a centuries old process and the Jirgas at a local level; however, the goal of the Afghan government is to establish the rule of law by creating legal entities such as courts, judges, and prosecutors to assist the development of the country's legal system. So the strong possibility exist that the 81 percent depicted probably is not an accurate representation of districts such as Bermal, and therefore the government of Afghanistan is still failing at their mission of providing rule of law to this community.

Reestablish Essential Services

In 2006-2007, as part of a substantial development push in the Bermal district and with assistance of coalition forces, the government of Afghanistan planned, funded and constructed a school to provide a facility for the communities in the immediate vicinity of the Bermal district center, in an effort to fill the void of education in the area. In 2011, while conducting an assessment of the community and services available, coalition forces accompanied by District Governor Hajji Zaher ventured to the school. Accompanying them were several local residents that had come to speak to the DGOV. Prior to the visit, the assessment team was told that the school was not operational and had never been in its four years of existence. The structure was now being used as quarters for ANP personnel, whose police headquarters was 100 meters north of this structure (DAT-Bermal 2012).

The story would continue to unfold as the then district governor and coalition forces spoke to the entourage of tribesmen accompanying them. The Bermal school in question along with an abandoned and never used clinic share walls with the district center and the ANA compound, which in turn shares walls and access with the coalition forces' operations outpost. All the tribesmen in attendance on this visit were in agreement that this location was the main reason children did not attend school. With the proximity to the Pakistani border of 7-8 kilometers, and a known heavy influence of insurgency in the area, tribesmen were not willing to send their children to schools, or to visit clinics or any facility provided by the central government. The number of reasons for the failure of

69

this particular school and clinic could be many, but one of the primary reasons given by the residents was because of the reality of insurgent retaliation towards any one that supports the government facilities, this as an effect of the lack of security in the district.

An additional concern in this same topic is the efficiency and capacity of the providers of these services or contractors. As is common practice when a contract is awarded to a construction company in Eastern Afghanistan, a sub-contractor is utilized, and at times a subcontractor two or three levels further removed, as in this case. Because the Bermal community's lack of resources to compete for these contracts, an outside source was used. Waziristan has always been considered a high-risk area, so, as a contractor enters the area and looks for a location to build, he will most likely always err on the side of safety and build the school, clinic, or whatever structure as close as he can to coalition forces or local law enforcement or military. One would think that provincial- and national-level oversight and supervision might mitigate these types of problems; however if the district governor or a provincial representatives make a decision for the location of these facilities without consulting with the community leaders, even if the contractor placed the structure where he was instructed to build it, it still not completely certain that this location is where the community needs this capacity. It also does not mitigate the problem of lack of coordination and community involvement in these types of decisions (DAT-Bermal 2012).

In April 2011, shortly after arriving, new Bermal DGOV Hajji Zaher, following the suggestion of coalition forces advisors, requested the immediate fill of critical *Tashkiel* positions in his district. In May 2011, Mr. Shir Khan, a member of the Pipali clan from the Utmanzai Waziri, reported to Zaher with a letter from the Provincial

Director of Education appointing Shir Khan as the District Education Official. With Bermal having no operational schools or programs at the time, any action taken by Shir Khan could have been seen as a positive move. However, Shir Khan was not seen in the district center (where he was supposed to work from) again until October 2011 for only a couple of hours. He had developed no plan, no request and no positive efforts for education in Bermal. In November 2011, DGOV Hajji Zaher requested Shir Khan's dismissal from the provincial governor; as of early 2013, his dismissal could not be verified.

During the same period of time as the assignment of the new District Education Official, the DGOV also inquired about filling the position of Public Health Official, when he was emphatically told by Dr. Wali Gul (Provincial Director of Health) that his district had one, Dr. Shir Ali, who had been assigned to the district for over one year by this point. Just as the district education official, the public health official had been seen possibly once and with the same results, no government run health care facilities, programs or education was being pursued in Bermal in now his second year of assignment. Dr. Shir Ali's letter of dismissal was also submitted to the provincial governor at this time. According to the Paktika Governor's spokesperson Mukhlis Afghan, as of December 2012 verification of dismissals, and new position fills was still unverified.

The problem pertaining to the delivery of services in the region was not only an issue at the district level to the villages, as efforts from the provincial- to the district-level were poorly executed and managed. In early 2012, due to consistent pressure from the newest Bermal DGOV, Dawlat Khan, and coalition forces advisors, new appointed

Provincial Director of Education Ata Mohammad Qany scheduled a visit to the district to assess the educational needs and visit a couple of locations reported as operational schools at the provincial- and national-level. Arriving late in the afternoon, Director Qany met with DGOV Dawlat Khan and advisors making plans for the next day's visit of the villages and schools. Early next morning coalition forces were notified that Qany had left the district on his way back to Sharana (Provincial Capital), without visiting any villages or schools, and leaving ANA and ANP units waiting to escort him. These actions reinforced the mistrust and lack of credibility the local Waziries harbor for government officials and policies.

The 2005-2010 Joint USAID-State Department Strategic Plan outlines several objectives in regards to the strategy to be implemented for Afghanistan. One of these objectives was the access to basic health care and primary education for 75 percent of all Afghans (USAID 2005, 11). As of June 2010 and according to the USAID Afghanistan profile, approximately 64 percent of the Afghan population had access to health services (USAID 2010). Based on a 2006 provincial profile done about the Paktika Province by the Central Statistics Office of Afghanistan, at the time the Paktika Province had 296 schools with 78,849 students, 18 health centers and three hospitals (MRRD 2007, 7). While these percentages are very encouraging and valid in many regions of Afghanistan, personal accounts, visits, and inspections of the Bermal region by coalition forces continued to reflect up to late 2012 that education nor health care provide by government programs was been executed in the area.

The percentages reported on the table shown below, along with similar data reported in 2008 by surveys conducted by the Asia Foundation, were based once again on a base number 6,348 people surveyed, and once again after doing the provincial and district mathematical breakdown the result is 39 people per district surveyed. According to the survey, 73 percent of the people in the East think that "Availability of education for children" in their area is very good or quite good, in comparison to 44 percent reported in 2008. It also reflects that 57 percent think that "Availability to clinics and hospitals" in their area is very good or quite good, which in 2008 was only 42 percent (Asia Foundation 2008, 61). The fact to underscore is that in 2011 in the Bermal district there was no government operated or supported clinics or schools. The only facilities available were private establishments (some in Pakistan), which the population had to pay individually for its services, and had no connection to the central government and along with that no funding or support from the state. The table also reflects many positive numbers and progress in other regions to include an 82 percent availability of clean water for the Eastern region. This definitely portrays the progress ongoing throughout Afghanistan, however the same personal accounts, visits, and inspections by coalition forces note that this percent does not represent the Bermal district or corresponding villages (DAT-Bermal 2012).

The status provided by these reports creates a generalization that if not identified could lead to a misguided update to the GoA along with ISAF mentors and evaluators who depend on this data being as correct as possible to continue to make decisions regarding the district. In its raw data the Asia Foundation divulged that in their 2012 Survey of the Afghan People, no districts in the Paktika Province were surveyed and in 2011 only one district in this same province was surveyed (not Bermal).

Securing the Populace

The Bermal district is a relatively small region in the Eastern Paktika Province

with a shared border with the NWFP of Pakistan. However, throughout 2011 despite its

small size, Bermal maintained a robust Afghan National Security Force, which included a

Kandak (battalion) of ANA that while not at full strength, amounted to several hundred

soldiers. The security of Bermal was also the responsibility of the ANP assigned to the

district whose authorized strength is 65, which during the same time frame fluctuated

between 50 percent to 75 percent of the personnel assigned actually present for duty. The

National Directorate of Security element assigned to this district, while experienced and

skilled, was devastatingly shorthanded and under supervised.

Putting aside the Ministry of Interior (MoI) initiative of recruiting, training and

implementation of ALP for now, as it will be discussed shortly. In 2011 the consensus amongst Paktika provincial leadership to include the provincial chief of police and governor was that the Bermal district was fully capable of securing itself. This determination came from only considering the number of ANSF assigned and present at any given time in the region; however, quantity does not equate to quality. The quality of the security forces in Eastern Paktika that are being referenced by this analysis is not only assessed on skill levels, but also on the overall selection of not only individuals but entire units whose characters and belief systems clash with the very people they are charged with protecting.

The Bermal ANP element was selected and moved from the district of Gomal, also part of the Paktika Province, in April 2011. While no official documentation was ever provided justifying the move, several provincial sources to include the Provincial Chief of Police Gen. Dawlat Khan insisted that the move had been made based on the positive performance of the unit in Gomal, hoping that they could duplicate their efforts in the high risk area of Bermal. The decision to relocate this specific unit was made in order to combat the poor performance of the previous police element in the Bermal district, which had even fewer personnel available and was by its own right being transferred to yet another location. Almost from the onset of their time at Bermal, the Gomal unit started having difficulties engaging and connecting with the community. The almost 100 percent *Tajik* police force from Gomal was intolerant of the *Pashtun* community; likewise, the not only *Pashtun* but deeply engrained Waziri clans were reluctant to deal with and in many ways defiance of the outsiders. The animosity among the community grew even more as a result of the police force's inability to even communicate with the tribesmen, as over 90 percent of the policemen spoke only Dari in a Pashtun area dominated by Pashtun speakers. Pashtun and Waziri Pashtun are different dialects in this region of Afghanistan that created yet another barrier between the law enforcement representatives of the government and the population (DAT-Bermal 2012).

The lack of trust from the Utmanzai Waziri towards the national police went further downhill due to no community policing, illegal taxation, questionable detention of citizens, and no protection from insurgent influence in the immediate area to include the district's bazaar located approximately 400 meters from the police headquarters (Lindsay 2012). In a December 2011 assessment of the Bermal ANP, a representative of the security services sub-branch of DYNCORP International, reported that the Bermal police was fewer than 30% trained in basic police requirements and was lacking logistical support from the provincial headquarters (Croft 2011).

While ANA *Kandak* assigned to Bermal changed the perspective of security efforts and provided another set of measures of performance, it did very little to change the overall effectiveness of securing the community and in some instances created more complex problems. Unfamiliarity with the region and its habitants provided one of the first issues for the ANA to confront. Relocating from the Nangarhar Province to Bermal in the Paktika Province in early 2011 proved to be a struggle from the beginning. Similar to the police force's adjustment, the Army had to make adjustments to a Waziri population known for their independent mindset and their resistance to foreign control (DAT-Bermal 2012). Also similar to the police element in Bermal, the army *Kandak* was replacing a unit that had fallen out of grace with the community, and the command. After five years in Bermal, the previous *Kandak* had become tired, corrupt to an alarming level and most important had alienated the community even further from the central

76

government. The new *Kandak* falling onto the same disruptive pattern continued the alienation of the community. With language once again becoming an issue from the beginning, interaction and the ability to understand internal clan dynamics, resulted in their attempts to "secure" to be a great challenge. They did not gain the trust of the local population, which was and continues to be a critical requirement to progress in this region and within a counterinsurgency. Instead, ANA elements resorted to strong arming the public, confiscation of property and detention of anyone they determined "suspicious." Their concerns only magnified as a result of the lack of brigade level assistance and support in key topics, resulting in the frequent dismissal or replacement of key leadership such as their Kandak commander, who in a period of six months was replaced four times.

The following tables are part of the 2011 survey of the people of Afghanistan by the Asia Foundation, in order to provide a sense of the mood and direction of the country, and a view of the current Afghan perception on key topics. However, Bermal is a highly insecure, dangerous, border district full of insurgents, and not represented in the survey as in 2011 only one district was surveyed in the Paktika province (not Bermal). Consequently, attitudes toward ANSF are harsher than in the rest of the country, which coalition forces can attest to with continual reports coming out of the Bermal region which would reflect drastic differences to the tables discussed below.

The silver lining in the security realm are the efforts of the ALP program that flourished in some areas of Eastern Paktika to include Southern Bermal, in the unofficial district of Shkin. The ALP is the evolution of several other attempts to empower the local tribes and leadership to basically facilitate the tribesmen to protect and secure their own villages. In August 2010 with assistance, training and logistical support from the government, local (village level) security forces started making a positive push towards the security of key areas of the country. These elements while becoming part of the overall government effort through the program, and legitimized by the MoI stamp as its initiator, were able to gain recognition and legitimacy as official locally selected police (L'Etoile 2011). Very similar to the *Kassadars* initiative of the British Empire, the ALP program, empowers the villages, tribes and population within those tribes, to take ownership of their own security, and provides some resources (funding) to do so. However, progress in the Bermal Central and Northern valley continued to be minimal with pushback from the main clans in the Utmanzai tribe. One of the main reasons for this resistance to the program is the lack of leadership at the local government level and the lack of border security in Eastern Bermal, making any clan attempting to initiate efforts a target. Without completely controlling the border, many of the elders state that, while ALP can provide some of their security needs, their proximity to the border makes them very easy targets to insurgents. Their solution has continuously been "if you shut down the border, we will provide ALP." In their own exaggerated manner the community leaders were asking for ANSF to provide the security and safety they would need in order to be more involved in government programs without fear of retaliation from criminal and insurgent elements operating in the region and making their home across the border (DAT-Bermal 2012).

As of 16 October 2012 the Afghan National Security Forces had reached an unprecedented number of 337,187 of uniformed defenders (ISAF 2012). The estimates are that by July 2013 the population of Afghanistan will reach 31,108,077; with 75 percent still living in the rural areas of the country (Central Intelligence Agency 2013).

Just as through the rest of the country, the ability to secure the population and region in Bermal is not a question of density of forces, but more of one of capabilities and training of those forces, along with the will to perform their duties.

Table 4.	GoA Program Results in the Bermal District		
Desired Effect (Criteria)	MOP	MOE	Effect Attained Y/N: Why?
Identifying the True Leaders	Establishment of the ASOP by the GoA.	Identification of 35 members ASOP Shura, monthly meetings on record.	N: ASOP Shura members not the true leaders of the community, no decisions made at Shuras.
Reestablishing Justice	No attempt at establishing legal court system in Bermal.	N/A	N: No legal mechanism to adjudicate criminal or civil cases.
Reestablish Essential Services	Assignment of Agricultural, Educational and Health Officials.	Number of programs, initiatives and projects initiated by officials.	N: No programs, initiatives or projects were initiated or proposed.
Securing the Populace	Assignment of new ANP unit, and ANA Kandak to the district.	Increase number of security personnel in the district.	N: Increase number of personnel did not increase patrols, but it did increase ANSF acts of corruptions against the community members.

Source: Created by author.

CHAPTER 5

CONCLUSIONS AND RECOMMENDATIONS

Conclusions

You've got the clock but we have the time.

— Suriname Proverb

As the 2014 deadline for troop withdrawal and transition of responsibility from the international community to Afghan hands, the role of the Afghan leaders from the capital to its most remote villages' representatives becomes critical. Focusing on the Enduring Strategic Partnership Agreement, the international community is now expecting that the Afghan leaders and people will step forward into their role to take ownership, emphasizing the sovereignty that is so important for their further development with the adequate support of the international community.

Amongst the key provisions of the agreement are the strengthening of Afghan institutions and governance and the advancing of long-term security (The White House 2012). It is without question that the development and advancement of security is where everything must begin or continue to improve to address the challenges in Afghanistan. However, without the trust of the population, and the ability of the GoA to legitimize itself and validate itself in the community's eyes, stability will continue to be illusive, for critical rural areas like Bermal, which in turn will result in continued instability in many regions and the inability of Afghanistan to move forward with its development.

<u>Identifying and Recruiting the True Leaders</u>

Engaging in a heated discussion with the Bermal District Governor and Afghan Security Forces leaders, *Mullah* Kuduz, a local religious leader from the *Pipali* tribe (a clan of the Utmanzai-Waziri tribe) that controls part of the Eastern region of the Paktika Province, explained to them one of the reasons most of his tribesmen and members of other nearby communities do not support the government is because, "you (Afghan Government and Coalition Forces) selected and emplaced jingle truck drivers and many other nobodies to make up these Shuras and represent the community not even verifying that they were the true leaders and representatives of these communities" (DAT-Bermal 2012). The previous example is one of many similar conversations, thoughts, and feelings displayed by the Afghan community and leadership in Bermal and nearby areas. The first criteria of evaluation, the "Identification and recruitment of local leaders and organizational representatives" (Department of the Army 2007, 156), meets the critical requirement for an accepted and trusted government mechanism by the community. The selection of the true leaders of the community, just as in the national-level, is a critical aspect of the development of the governance mechanism. Leaders that the people will actually follow can provide the require proper influence to assist the involvement and engagement of other key leaders and the population in general. This consequently leading to local development and further advance the eventual end state of a stable community.

Many distinctive and similar arguments can be made regarding the strategies and courses of action addressed in chapter 4 regarding the importance of the selection of leaders to stabilize a region. The need for familiarity, trust, similarities, and over all connection to a leader is in essence the same throughout the world. While in the United

States, city, state and national leaders come from any part of the country, the rural, small towns and cities continue to be managed and lead by locals. Generations of local leaders, law enforcement and community members are the driving force behind these inner cultures and governance mechanism. People generally want to select their leaders from their community. They want leaders who are like them, speak their language, know their customs. They want leaders who understand their concerns and respond to them, and who can be held accountable for their time in office. Now put that same mold on a village in one of the most secluded regions in the world, in one of the most primitive countries in the world and you get not only resistance; but a resistance grown from distrust, unfamiliarity and defiance, as outside rules and rulers are forced into this society. It is no wonder the residents of Bermal are so dissatisfied with their leadership.

Whether it is the assignment of non-local provincial or district chiefs by the South Vietnamese government to assist the pacification and promote the region's control, or the selection of *Maliks* by the British government to impose their will in Waziristan, or the misguided selection of ASOP Shura members by GoA to reign in the Eastern Paktika tribes, the results in all three cases while varied in levels of failure. They also share the similar theme of feeding the distrust of the central government by the local population, and add to the alienation of these same communities by the use of outsiders to control unstable regions (unstable by their standards).

The selection of *Maliks* by the British/Indian Government in Waziristan in the late 1800s, early 1900s did provide a manner of maintaining situational awareness of issues, and arising problems for the government. However it also restricted their ability to affect changes, or control over the Waziri, as it was openly known that the *Maliks* were the

83

government and therefore their power in most regions was merely cosmetic. This same sentiment is comparable to the intentional assignment of out of the area district chiefs to districts through South Vietnam by the GVN. By trying to create an environment for their chiefs, where favoritism and bias were minimized when making their decisions as district chiefs, the government alienated these leaders and themselves from the community. Similarly the establishment of ASOP Shuras by the GoA in 2008, along with the questionable selection of local district governors and district staff, just as in 1900 Waziristan or 1950 Vietnam created a false sense of connection to the population. Once again it introduced external entities into a close knitted, family and tribal community, which created a gap of distrust and illegitimacy for the Afghan government in many districts and villages, to include the Bermal district.

It is critical to note that there is no substitute for provincial and national leadership involvement at the local level in such districts as Bermal. The community's issues must be presented and addressed at a higher level with some sort of feedback presented to them. While currently Bermal is still fighting to advance with any major development due to the security situation and the very difficult tribal dynamics and pushback from the tribes towards the GoA, keeping them in seclusion and cutting them off from any guidance or support will continue to increase the problems which eventually the provincial level will have to deal with.

Another reason for the Bermal area's reluctance to become part of the greater GoA is a result of the failure of the provincial- and national-level government to identify viable applicants for key positions that coincide with the centuries old self government mechanism that this community already uses. Trying to adapt Western (Kabul) style government mechanisms and criteria for selection of key leaders in this region, will continue to fail, due to the inability of this technique to provide acceptable candidates. The dismissal of key tribal leaders from holding required positions by the central government based on possible ties to Waziristan, Pakistan and questionable characters could be said to be naïve, since everyone is linked to everyone else by family or tribe in this region. Sometimes the best person to fill one of these positions is not the one the government wants, sometimes is not even the "good guy" if using Kabul criteria. Perhaps the GoA along with coalition forces "must recognize and continuously address that this 'The American way is best' bias is unhelpful" (Department of the Army 2007, 202).

Reestablish a Justice System

As part of an attempt to push the Bermal district governor Hajji Zaher to provide basic administrative services and guidance to the community, an effort was made by Bermal Shura members to bring forth local issues for him to adjudicate. One such dispute was the land dispute that had been in progress for months between two Utmanzai Waziri tribesmen, one from the Pipali clan and the other one from the Malikshay clan. Due to the discrepancy in wealth and tribal support, the Pipali clansman was in control of the land and had no intention of stepping back his efforts against the weaker and less supported Malikshay member. As expected, with poor knowledge of the tribal dynamics and little personal relationship with the Utmanzai clans, the district governor was limited in his attempts to assist in any manner. Furthermore, with an unfilled *Tashkiel* and no legal expert or equivalent at the district level, the dispute in question, as many others brought to light, went unresolved. So without a solution, the Malikshay tribesman, who was the person bringing forth the issue, left the district center unsatisfied.

Approximately six weeks later the Pipali clansman, who seemed to be more successful in resolving the dispute, was seen leaving the district center. When asked if the dispute had been settled, he acknowledged that he had had a change of heart, and he and the Malikshay clansman had settled the issue. At a later time, several local villagers reported to the DAT and coalition forces, and were confirmed by MAJ Mohammad Aslam, the district NDS chief, that the reason for the settlement of the dispute had been that both tribesmen were taken to Miran Shah on the Pakistan side of the Durand Line where the matter was settled by Taliban leadership. Regardless if it was Taliban leadership, Waziri tribal leaders, or both who settled the disagreement, the fact of the matter was that it was settled outside the Afghan government, highlighting the lack of local governance and rule of law (DAT-Bermal 2012). This latest example is representative of the second criteria chosen to evaluate the effectiveness of a local government "Reestablish justice system," as it applies to stability and counterinsurgency efforts (Department of the Army 2007, 156).

Just as selection of the leaders has a key role in the development of an effective government, the establishment or reestablishment of a judicial system further fills a need and requirement for the community by the local government. This requirement assists the government to obtain the legitimacy it needs and provides a vehicle to affect changes in the population as to their support and relationship with the local governmental leaders. The judicial system and its sub-mechanisms in many aspects are the hybrid of government and military/law enforcement powers that the population sees. A corrupt or dysfunctional legal system discredits the government and its role of assisting the public, and simultaneously adds to the fear of uniformed personnel, be that of police or of the military, by the people.

Reverting back to the inability of the Afghan government to fill key *Tashkiel* positions at the district-level during the current conflict, damages and setbacks continue to add to the mistrust and fear created by the lack of a judicial system in Bermal district. There is something good to be said about not having a judicial system in place, rather than having a brutally corrupt and inefficient one; however in the case of the Bermal district or any district or region in a similar situation, absence opens the door to many other problems. The villages and communities that make up these areas do adhere to their centuries old methods of adjudication (*Sharia Law and Pashtunwali*). However efforts to regain or in many cases maintain control, insurgents and the regional shadow government has taken the absence of these central government systems as an opportunity to step in and fill the void. This shadow government with its traveling courts provides a sense of stability by adjudicating legal, moral, and cultural cases that are presented to them, and use their militant side to ensure the judgments are enforced, providing the population resolution, along with some type of fairness.

By comparison the British solution in the same region of Waziristan almost 100 years before was to just let it happen, let the tribal system rule, judge and punish itself as it had done up to that point. Ignoring the needs of the region in matters of providing legal venues was done on purpose as part of their policy of nonintervention. All the British/Indian efforts to introduce and enforce the Indian Penal Code were met with resistance and with no presence in the area other than the insignificant visits by the political agents, as their policy of nonintervention continued to meet with failure. This in turn possibly reinforced the distancing or unwieldiness of the tribes within Waziristan to connect to the government and continue to keep out a Western style judicial process for even longer. In contrast, the Government of South Vietnam's use of the Provincial Security Committees is an example of the methods and techniques that were planned and executed. The down side to these actions was the corruption and misuse that accompanied these attempts, which contributed to the further alienation of the South Vietnamese population from its government.

There is no question that insurgent and general criminal activities are some of the primary reasons for the need of a legal mechanism in Bermal. The legal reform in an area such as Bermal would also bring the legal professionals that would facilitate the mediation between parties, regarding property and civil disagreements. In the absence of this mediating party, the opportunity is left open once again for the shadow courts of insurgent groups operating in the district and nearby regions to gain popular support, and be seen as the providers of some sort of stability and fairness.

<u>Reestablish Essential Services</u>

After weeks of reports of illegal taxes being collected from jingle truck drivers hauling lumber through the Bermal bazaar by the Malikshay and Sifali clans of the Utmanzai Waziri, the district governor facilitated a meeting with these clans' leaders, along with the local law enforcement. Apart from being a violation of the GoA law to collect such taxes or tolls if not assigned as the district tax collector by the government, the additional concern was that these taxes were being used to support insurgents in the area with supplies or funds. During the meeting, one of the key Malikshay leaders, Hajji Dasta Gheer, was asked if he was aware of the collection of these "taxes". Without hesitation he confirmed his knowledge of such tolls. He continued to explain that the land on which the Bermal bazaar was situated was owned by the Malikshay and Sifali clans; therefore, a toll was charged to all trucks carrying wood conducting business or passing through their land. In any particular day approximately 250 to 300 truckloads of wood pass through the bazaar. Reportedly, each carried an average of $600 worth of wood (58,452 Pakistani Rupees). The fare being collected from each truck was 300 Rupees, equivalent to approximately $3, for which the truck drivers were given a receipt to confirm their compliance and ensure they do not get charged twice in the same day (DAT-Bermal 2012).

Hajji Dasta Gheer was then asked if this money was used to assist the insurgent fighters and activity in the area. His response, while vague, did give some credence to the allegation. He explained that the community could not operate and live safely in this area without paying for their protection. The payment of certain fees to Miran Shah (city in Pakistan, linked to insurgent activities) permitted them to continue to operate shops in the bazaar, pay for the settlement of disputes, and allow them safe passage across the border. An additional aspect that he and all the tribe members present agreed on was that the funds collected provided critical necessities for their clan, tribe and community. The funds collected assisted with medications, doctors' bills and transportation to medical facilities when needed (as Bermal does not have any operational government clinics or pharmacies) along with paying for funeral and burial costs of clan members. These funds also provided the means for clan and tribal leaders to travel to Sharana (Provincial Capital) or to Kabul to address essential issues with government officials, along with assisting families to pay for schools across the border for the tribe's children to attend, since no operational schools exist in the Bermal district. So with no enforcement capabilities to stop the collection of these "taxes," this practice continued (DAT-Bermal 2012).

"Reestablishing essential services provided by local government, to include educational and medical capacity" (Department of the Army 2007, 156) is without a doubt a critical aspect of the government's ability to build trust, credibility and fulfill critical needs of its communities. As of December 2012 the Bermal district had no schools or medical facilities provided or supported by the government. For this reason, the community had to meet these requirements, and they viewed the government as non-existent (DAT-Bermal 2012).

The criterion to view and evaluate an effective government mechanism of the establishment or reestablishment of essential services was not chosen at random. The importance of social services rank just below providing security and safety for the population. With the center of gravity for success in an insurgency being the population, its welfare and the support it displays for the insurgents or the counterinsurgents is the foundation for a long term victory. Communities, who are given no support and no attention by the government and see no benefit in supporting an absentee government, consequently realize that they have nothing to lose by not supporting nor participating. On the other hand, by merely showing submission to the insurgent elements in the region, they maintain whatever minimal support and stability they do have along with possibly their lives.

Unable or unwilling to push forward into the nonintervention areas of the NWFP, the British/Indian government suffered the consequences when they attempted to initiate a more forward policy in that region. Their attempt to win the communities over with schools, clinics and other services that could have promoted a possible bridge between the tribes and the government was hampered by several self-imposed restrictions. While some of these restriction were due to the inability to provide a long term solution with the poorly resourced services, the lack of security was the key factor for the forward policy failure. The lack of presence in Waziristan from the onset of the annexation of the Punjab, assisted in the status of lawlessness and lack of security, which in turn affected the ability to promote development, and fed the mistrust and alienation of not only the Waziri tribesmen towards the government but from the government towards the population in general.

The British Vietnam government efforts in their distinctive time periods are similar with the distinction of the continual security push by the GVN in regards to its hamlets. While the government of South Vietnam's Strategic Hamlet initiative and the subsequent United States (CORDS) programs met many setbacks and criticisms, their ability to continue to push for presence in the rural areas and make available some of the critical social services to the population was not a total failure. In the early 1970s, CORDS and Civil Affairs operations that promoted these programs were only one portion of the total counterinsurgency effort in the overall flawed strategy for the Vietnam War, as the US was initiating the exit from the region. By 1970 93 percent of South Vietnam villages were reported to be living in relative security, which in turn allowed for the increase of social services (White 2009). "The greatest success of the CORDS program was that it not only established effective interagency coordination, but also succeeded in convincing the military to incorporate development projects into its overall security strategy" (White 2009).

In 2012 the district of Bermal gave the appearance of been an economy of force effort for the province and national governments of Afghanistan. While security in the district continues to be a major obstacle for any attempt at any type of major development the ignoring of key and basic services required of the community by the Afghan government only feeds the anti-government sentiment and opens the doors to a small, but determined, and present shadow government. It is possible that the ignoring of this region by the government can be attributed to the many erroneous reports being delivered to the provincial and national-level in regards to the district's status. However, in view of the lack of security and immense amounts of problems in the district, it is very possible that the GoA views Bermal as a problem without solution, or one to which the resources and commitment is not currently available. That being the case, a complete re-assessment of the region, with actual higher level government officials visiting schools, clinics and critical social service sites in the district, would give the central government a true status of the current development status of Bermal. Otherwise it would seem that the centuries old policy of nonintervention is still in effect.

Securing the Populace "The Key"

In chapter 2 insurgency was defined as: "an organized movement aimed at the overthrow of a constituted government through the use of *subversion and armed conflict.*" The methods clearly described for the execution of an insurgency were *subversion and armed conflict.* So with this definition the assumption is that violence, and consequently the mitigation of that violence or *Security* must be, if not the critical aspect, then one of the primary ones for mounting a counterinsurgency.

In 2011, the Bermal district did manage to convene their ASOP-initiated Shura. However, this Shura was composed of midlevel tribal representatives from the Sifali and Pipali clans of the Utmanzai Waziri tribe. That being the case, it is also fair to say that all these midlevel representatives did, for the most part, report the meeting notes, status and important issues to the higher level leaders in their respective communities. Because of the lack of an agenda and overall services provided or initiatives for projects from the government, these notes and information never amounted to much; nevertheless the information was getting back to the tribal leaders. One such mid-level leader and messenger was Gul Swab Khan from the Sifali clan, the ASOP Shura appointed Shura Chief, who did speak out on important issues raised by the tribes.

Frequently as more important issues came up, the DGOV would ask for some of these leaders to make a special visit to the district center to address them; in most cases, it was due to the persistence of coalition forces' advisors. During one such visit on August 15, 2011, tribal representative Gul Swab Khan was asked to meet with the DGOV regarding military operations affecting the logging areas near and their affect on the lumber industry critical to Bermal. The meeting lasted just over one hour during the later part of the afternoon, with no major solutions or decisions being made. Gul Swab Khan and a few other tribal members that accompanied him to the meeting from his village, approximately 14 kilometers north of the district center, left soon after the conclusion of the *Shura*. As he traveled back to his village mid-way through the route his vehicle was stopped by what was reported later to be insurgents, who identified Gul Swab Khan as the Bermal district center Shura Chief and murdered him. This assassination (by no means the first or last of its type) underscored the danger of serving as a government official in an area largely controlled by, or populated by, insurgents. In the subsequent district meetings, the issue of selecting a new chief was always met with resistance by all clans in the region, with the reoccurring message: why participate and get involved even further, when the result was always broken promises, no action, and risk of assassination; "So if we do not participate, and get nothing from you (which we were not, anyway), we have lost nothing and we keep our families from being killed." This created a void in the Shura Chief position, which as of December 2012 was still vacant.

The last criteria used for this analysis is in many aspects possibly one of the most important ones and one of the most elusive; *securing the populace continuously.* As described in FM 3-24, counterinsurgency efforts should start by "controlling key areas and providing continuous security for the local populace" (Department of the Army 2006, 174). Which most likely assist in developing the support needed for the local government in this (or any) region, which subsequently creates a spark for development and economic growth, which in turn must be secured and safeguarded.

"A secure operating environment is a prerequisite for any successful pacification effort" (White 2009). Just as in any other military operation, it would seem that the theme keeps returning to security as the pivotal point for effective governance, which in turn enables a functional and effective judicial system and advances the economic and social development of a community. It would also seem that the modern district of Bermal might as well be the same Waziristan that the British and Indian government had the misfortune to try to manage and control in the late 1800s. The similarities and unwillingness to intervene are only interrupted briefly because of the moments of forced intervention quite often directed or initiated by coalition forces in current times and the British a century ago.

While the British policy of nonintervention served well to contain the lawlessness and troubles of Waziristan, it also hindered their ability to affect any future for the Empire in that region. The use of local security forces (*Kassadars*) was successful for the region, but only because these elements were not really supervised or made to adhere to the British/Indian law codes. *Kassadar* elements just as the *Maliks* and anybody that operated constantly in the zone of nonintervention were left to conduct themselves as tribal assets, which in many ways did not change the manner in which the tribes would conduct themselves, as their protection remained in their own hands as it had for centuries prior.

While the Bermal district today is not consider a zone of nonintervention, the perceived neglect by the central government has created many of the same conditions the British dealt with 100 years ago. Bermal does not lack the security personnel to execute its mission, with a *Kandak* of ANA and a police force that is manned as a medium level district, its ability to provide the continual security of the population is very much within their capacity. However, the capabilities of these forces, their skill levels and most important the will to provide that security, to basically do their job are the critical aspects lacking in their ability to secure the region. In a 2009 report the RAND Corporation depicted that Pashtuns in general make up a proportional number of members of the ANA as compared to the Afghan Pashtun population, approximately 40 percent (Younossi 2009, 21). However it continues to be surprising that Shkin supported ALP efforts are the

95

only source of local volunteers, recruits and support for security efforts in the Bermal district, leaving the GoA in many occasions no chose but to assigned ANSF from other ethnic, and tribal groups to the region.

As the Regional Forces and Popular Forces did for South Vietnam, continual presence and engagement of the community by population focused, trustworthy and trained security forces could alleviate and improve the alienation currently felt by the Bermal residents towards the government and its representatives. While the use of elements such as the Afghan Local Police brings forward the ownership and participation of the community to be involved in their own security, the ultimate responsibility is that of the government's assigned security forces and government overall. Table 5 briefly summarizes the analysis presenting the consideration that presence is one of the critical aspect of success or failure in the absence of it, for a complex problem as are insurgencies. "The U.S. military will never be able to create government structures capable of winning popular support if the indigenous government is inherently defective and corrupt" (White 2009).

Table 5. Case Study Comparison (Effect Attained Y/N: Why?)				
Case/Criteria	Identifying the True Leaders	Reestablishing Justice	Reestablish Essential Services	Securing the Populace
British in Waziristan	N: Lack of influence/presence	N: Lack of influence/presence	Y: Increase presence	N: Lack of presence
Vietnam 1950s and 60s	N: Government Corruption	N: Government Corruption	Y: Continuous Presence	Y: Continuous Presence
ISAF in Afghanistan	N: Lack of influence/presence	N: Lack of influence/presence	N: Lack of influence/presence	N: Lack of supervision and Corruption

Source: Created by author.

The relevance of the LLO of governance and its inherent tasks or objectives continues to be valid as reflected in the case studies presented in chapter 4. While the combination of criteria can be subjective and can vary from analysis to analysis, the validity of its effectiveness and place within the counterinsurgency methodology is critical. However all the criteria or objectives and the desire end state require an important elements, action. Action for the purpose of this analysis is the physical presence and involvement of the Afghan government, action to make decisions and select the correct leaders, action to reestablish the justice system, action to reestablish essential services, and action to secure the populace. A simple recommendation to a complex problem is, that involvement and physical presence is the initial and most important step to address the challenges associated with the poor effectiveness of governance and stability in the Bermal district.

As coalition forces and the international community relinquishes and prepares to transfer authority to the GoA by the end of 2014; history once again echoes the a similar sound, bringing forth the lessons of the publicized withdrawal of US forces from Vietnam and the Vietnamization policy that preamble this withdrawal. The parallel between both exit strategies bring about the question; if the same unfortunate result is in the future of the Afghanistan conflict. The ideology maintained for the success of the Afghan government is that by working to strengthen their military capabilities as the US did for the South Vietnamese Army; that the ANSF will take responsibility and control of their own security and defense with effectively. However, as it was in the case of the South Vietnamese security forces, the Afghan forces while increasing their numbers are still in the infancy of their military development.

The publicized withdrawal in 2014, once again appears to create an opportunity in this case for *Taliban*/insurgent elements to wait for the departure of coalition forces, while planning the continuation of their antigovernment activities once the ISAF opposition is gone. The anticipated outcome can be argued will mimic the eventual fall of South Vietnamese to the North Vietnamese forces in 1975. Regions like the Bermal district, with no intervention or presence by the GoA while they counted with the support of coalition forces, will sink even further into the zone of nonintervention that has been know as, with now only Afghan forces and officials available.

Epilogue

It would be absurd to attempt to pinpoint a reason for stability failures for the British in Waziristan during their struggles in the late 1800s early 1900s, or the disputed withdrawal of American troops without achieving victory in Vietnam in the 1960s, just as it would be irresponsible to ignore all the progress coalition efforts have made in recent years in reference to the stability and development of Afghanistan post *Taliban*. However, an honest and unbiased review of critical regions such as the Bermal district and Eastern Paktika must be made in order to understand some of the very real and dangerous challenges the Government of Afghanistan and any coalition or external assistance is and will be facing in order to make a true effort at not only providing an effective governance mechanism, but overall stability.

The case studies in this analysis were addressed briefly, to highlight focal points of the challenges experienced, and their solutions to those challenges. The brevity of their input in this analysis at their particular times and locations was purposeful, as it would have required a detailed and more in depth analysis of each one to fully address the history, and consequences of their outcomes. A final observation can be argued, that the failure of governance in the Bermal district is due to the perception that Bermal is not Afghanistan, as it is ignored and treated by the GoA as "no man's land." Bermal is also not Pakistan, and as such Pakistan maintains its distance and keeps its hands away. Bermal is Waziristan, and is governed as such. Without the true leaders to follow, without acceptable laws to guide it, without community needs being met, and without security and protection, governance in the Bermal district will continue to be nonexistent.

GLOSSARY

Amir. A prince, commander, or head of state in some Islamic countries.

Chieu Hoi. Meaning "open arms," a reintegration program for VCI and North Vietnamese soldiers to voluntarily return to the side of GVN.

Darajat. A cultural region of central Pakistan, located in the region where the provinces of Balochistan, Khyber Pakhtunkhwa and Punjab meet.

Fakir. An Islamic holy man.

Jirga. A Pashto term for an assembly of male elders where decisions are made and disputes between rival parties are resolved.

Kandak. An Army battalion (unit size).

Kassadar. Waziristan resident civil armed forces (tribal policeman).

Kharoti. A Pashtun tribe of Ghilzai origin.

Malik. King, chieftain. It is very similar to the Arabic name/ word mālik, which in some languages means "master" or head (of something).

Mullah. An Islamic holy man.

Mujahedeen. A military force of Muslim guerilla warriors.

Nang. Pashtun word for honor.

Pashtun. An Iranic ethnic group belonging to Afghanistan and Pakistan.

Pashtunwali. A non-written ethical code and traditional lifestyle which the indigenous Pashtun people follow.

Shura. The Arabic word for consultation. A meeting of where tribes select leaders and make major decisions.

Tajik. An ethnic group in Tajikistan, Afghanistan, Uzbekistan, Iran, Russia and China.

Taliban. From Persian *ṭālibān*, plural of *ṭālib* 'student, seeker of knowledge', from Arabic (so named because the movement reputedly began amongst Afghani students exiled in Pakistan).

Tashkera. Official Afghan government identification card.

Tashkiel. List and organization representing a predetermine structure; as the staff requirements for a government entity or personnel and equipment requirement for another government/military organization.

Tehrik-i-Taliban Pakistan. An umbrella organization of various Islamist militant groups based in the northwestern Federally Administered Tribal Areas along the Afghan border in Pakistan.

Waziri. Pashtun tribe settled in the North Waziristan and South Waziristan agencies of Pakistan, and FR Bannu and parts of Tank.

APPENDIX A

INTERVIEW SUBJECTS FOR THE BERMAL DISTRICT STUDY

Name	Position	Date and Type of Interview	Time Frame in Afghanistan
LTC Eric Lindsay	Security Transition Team Chief, Bermal District, Paktika Province	Writen-07 January 2013	2011-2012
CPT Nicole Alexander	Civil Affairs Team 224 Team Leader, Paktika Province	Writen-08 January 2013	2011-2012
Lisa Arthur	USAID Field Program Officer, Paktika Province	Writen-06 January 2013	2011-2012

REFERENCE LIST

411th Engineer Brigade Brief. 2010. http://411enbde.net/G2//training/Afghanistan-Threat. 10 April (accessed 20 April 2013).

Afghanistan Ministry of Rural Rehabilitation and Development (MRRD). 2007. Paktika province profile. Compiled by the National Area-Base Development Program (NABDP). http://www.mrrd.gov.af/nabdp, Kabul (accessed 12 April 2013).

Afghanistan Official Gazette (AOG) No 855. 2011. Law of firearms, ammunition and explosives. Afghanistan Criminal Law Code (1384). www.lexadin.nl/wlg/legis/nofr/oeur/lxweaf.htm (accessed 12 April 2013).

Afghanistan Strategy Secretariat. 2011. *Afghanistan national development strategy.* Kabul, Afghanistan: Strategy Secretariat.

Andrade, Dale, and James H. Willbanks, LTC, U.S. Army, Retired. 2006. CORDS/Phoenix: Counterinsurgency lessons from Vietnam for the future. *Military Review* (March-April 2006): 9-23.

Arthur, Lisa. Paktika province, Afghanistan field program officer. 2011. Email interview by author. 6 January 2013.

Barfield, Thomas, and Neamatollah Nojumi. 2010. Bringing more effective governance to Afghanistan: 10 pathways to stability. *Middle East Policy* 17, no. 4 (Winter): 40-52.

Bennet, Lieutenant Colonel Mark J. *Pacification operations in Vietnam.* Canadian Forces College, Canada, 2011.

Britannica Online Encyclopedia. 2013a. Anglo-Afghan wars (British-Afghani history). www.britannica.com (accessed 12 November 2012).

———. 2013b. Vietnam: State and society in pre-colonial Vietnam. www.britannica.com (accessed 17 February 2013).

Bruce, Lieutenant Colonel C. E. 1938. *Waziristan, 1936-1937: The problems of the north-west frontiers of India and their solutions.* Aldershot, England: Gale & Polden, Wellington Works.

Casper, Cpt. Robert, USMC. 2012 Acceptable corruption: is there such a thing, or are we fooling ourselves? *Marine Corps Gazette.* www.mca-marines.org (accessed 12 April 2013).

Central Intelligence Agency. 2012. World Fact Book: Afghanistan. www.cia.org, (accessed 15 April 2012).

Chayes, Sarah. 2007. *The punishment of virtue*. London: Penguin Books.

Coll, Steve. 2004. *Ghost wars: The secret history of the CIA, Afghanistan and Bin Laden, from the Soviet invasion to September 10, 2001*. New York: Penguin Group.

Constable, Pamela. 2008. A modernized taliban thrives in Afghanistan: Militia operates a parallel government. *Washington Post Foreign Service*, 20 September.

Croft, Nelson. 2011. Task Force 2/28 Black Lions AUP Site Assessment. Security Services, DynCorp International, 4 December.

Department of the Army. 2007. Field Manual (FM) 3-24, *Counterinsurgency*. Washington, DC: Government Printing Office, December.

———. 2008. Field Manual (FM) 3-07, *Stability operations*. Washington, DC: Government Printing Office, December.

Department of Defense. 2012a. *National defense strategic guidance*. Washington, DC: Government Printing Office, January.

———. 2012b. Report on progress towards security and stability in Afghanistan: United States Plan for Sustainment the Afghanistan National Security Forces, USDoD, April.

———. 2012c. *Sustaining U.S. global leadership priorities for 21st century defense*. Washington, DC: Government Printing Office.

District Augmentation Team-Bermal (DAT-Bermal), MAJ Jorge Mendoza. 2011-12. *Daily reports and written Bermal overview*. April to April.

Filkins, Dexter. 2011. Review of *The wrong war: Grit, strategy, and the way out of Afghanistan* by Bing West. *The New York Times*. www.nytimes.com (accessed 14 April 2013).

Flynn, Michael MG, Director of Intelligence. 2009. State of the insurgency: Trends, intentions and objectives. Briefing, International Security Assistance Force, Afghanistan, U.S. Forces Afghanistan, 22 December.

Flynn, Michael T., Major General USA, Captain Matt Pottinger, USMC, and Paul D. Batchelor, DIA. 2010. Fixing intel: A blueprint for making intelligence relevant in Afghanistan. *Voices From the Field*, January.

Galula, David. 2006. *Pacification in Algeria: 1956-1958*. Arlington, VA: RAND Corporation.

———. 1964. *Counterinsurgency warfare: Theory and practice*, Westport, CT: Praeger Security International.

Gompert, David C. 2009. *Reconstruction under fire: Unifying civil and military counterinsurgency.* Santa Monica, CA: RAND Corporation.

Gonzalez, Robert J. 2009. *American counterinsurgency: Human science and human terrain.* Chicago: Prickly Paradigm Press.

Grau, Lester, W. 1996. *The bear went over the mountain: Soviet tactics in Afghanistan.*, Fort Leavenworth, KS: Foreign Military Studies Office.

Gul, Imtiaz. 2009. *The most dangerous place: Pakistan's lawless frontier.* New York: Penguin Books.

Heeg, Jason. 2011. *Insurgency in Balochistan.* Fort Leavenworth, KS: The Foreign Military Studies Office.

Hunt, Richard A. 1995. *Pacification: The American struggle for Vietnam's hearts and minds.* Oxford: Westiview Press.

Independent Directorate of Local Governance (IDLG). 2010. *Afghanistan sub-national governance policy.* Islamic Republic of Afghanistan: May 2010.

Information Dominance Center (IDC), ISAF Joint Command (IJC). 2012. *Model district: 110505:* 1-17, 22 February.

International Security Assistance Force (ISAF). 2013. *RC-East.* http://www.isaf.nato.int/ subordinate-commands/rc-east/index.php#AOR (accessed 10 January 2013).

Jalali, Ali Ahmad, and Lester W. Grau. 1995. *The other side of the mountain: Mujahedeen tactics in the Soviet-Afghan war.* Quantico, VA: The United States Marine Corps Studies and Analysis Division.

Joes, Anthony J. 2010. *Victorious insurgencies: Four rebellions that shaped our world.* Kentucky: The University Press of Kentucky.

Joint Command, Command Information Center. *Afghanistan model district document No. 110505,* 22 February 2012.

Jones, Seth G. 2008. *Counterinsurgency in Afghanistan.* Arlington, VA: RAND Corporation.

Kaim, Markus. 2011. *Es Fehlt Der Strategische Konsens.* Frankfurter Allgemeine, Zeitung.

Khyber.org. 2013. Tribal locations. http://www.khyber.org/images/maps/triballocations (accessed 11 February 2013).

Kilcullen, David. 2009. *The accidental guerrilla: Fighting small wars in the midst of a big one*. New York: Oxford University Press.

Komer, Robert W. 1970. *Organization and management of the "new model" pacification program 1966-1969*. Arlington. VA: RAND Corporation.

Leader Development Education for Sustained Peace (LDESP). 2012a. Af-Pak News update. 24 September 2012. https://www.ldesp.org (accessed 30 September 2012).

———. 2012b. Af-Pak News update: 8 October 2012. https://www.ldesp.org (accessed 12 October 2012).

———. 2012c. Af-Pak News Update: 23 October 2012. https://www.ldesp.org (accessed 28 October 2012).

L'Etoile, Joe. 2011. *Transforming the conflict in Afghanistan village stability operations/Afghan local police and bottom-up population mobilization.* McLean, VA: Orbis Operations.

Lindsay, LTC Eric, Task Force Black Lion Operations Officer and Security Transition Team Chief. 2012. Email interview by author. 7 January 2012.

Mahsud, Mansur Khan. 2010. *The battle for Pakistan: Militancy and conflict in south Waziristan*. Counterterrorism Strategy Initiative Policy Paper. Washington, DC: New America Foundation, April.

Marighella, Carlos. 1971. *For the liberation of Brazil*. Translated by John Butt and Rosemary Sheed. England: Penguin Books, Harmondsworth.

Mazikowski, CPT Nicole, Civil Affairs Team 224 Team Leader. 2013. Email interview by author. 8 January.

Melin, Major Nicholas, O. 2011. The challenge of access: Using road construction as a tool in counterinsurgency. Master's Thesis, Command and General Staff College, Fort Leavenworth, KS.

Moreman, T. R. 1998. *The Army in India and the development of frontier warfare, 1849-1947*. Great Britain: MacMillan Press.

Moyar, Mark. 2007. *Phoenix and the birds of prey: Counterinsurgency and counterterrorism in Vietnam*. Lincoln: University of Nebraska Press.

Naval Postgraduate School (NPS). 2011. Program for culture & conflict studies, Afghanistan administrative divisions: Afghanistan tribal map, www.nps.edu/programs/ccs (accessed 15 November 2011).

———. 2010. Who is who in the Pakistani Taliban: A Sampling of insurgent personalities in seven operational zones in Pakistan's Federally Administered Tribal Areas (FATA) and North Western Frontier Province. www.nps.edu/programs/ccs (accessed 21 April 2013).

Nola, Cpl. Zachary, Regimental Combat Team-7, 1st Marine Division Public Affairs. 2013. *Finding Afghan solutions for Afghan problems*. http://www.isaf.nato. int/article/news/finding-afghan-solutions-for-afghan-problems (accessed 9 January 2013).

Rashid, Ahmed. 2008. *Descent into chaos*. New York: Penguin Group.

———. 2012. *Pakistan on the brink: The Future of America, Pakistan, and Afghanistan*. London: Viking Penguin Publishing.

Rennie, Ruth. 2008. *A survey of the Afghan people: 2008*. Kabul: The Asia Foundation, Afghan Centre for Socio-economic and Opinion Research (ACSOR). http://asiafoundation.org (accessed 5 October 2012).

———. 2009. *A survey of the Afghan people: 2009*. Kabul: The Asia Foundation, Afghan Centre for Socio-economic and Opinion Research (ACSOR). http://asiafoundation.org (accessed 5 October 2012).

———. 2010. *A survey of the Afghan people: 2010*. Kabul: The Asia Foundation, Afghan Centre for Socio-economic and Opinion Research (ACSOR). http://asiafoundation.org (accessed 5 October 2012).

———. 2011. *A survey of the Afghan people: 2011*. Kabul: The Asia Foundation, Afghan Centre for Socio-economic and Opinion Research (ACSOR). http://asiafoundation.org (accessed 5 October 2012).

———. 2012. *A survey of the Afghan people: 2012*. Kabul: The Asia Foundation, Afghan Centre for Socio-economic and Opinion Research (ACSOR). http://asiafoundation.org (accessed 5 October 2012).

Roe, Andrew, M. 2010. *Waging war in Waziristan: The British struggle in the land of Bin Laden, 1849-1947*. Lawrence: University Press of Kansas.

———. 2011. What Waziristan means for Afghanistan. *Middle East. Quarterly* (Winter): 37-46.

The History Channel. 2013. Vietnamization. http://www.history.com/topics/ vietnamization (accessed 1 May 2013).

Tucker, Alexander L. P. 1921. *Sir Robert G. Sandeman: Peaceful conqueror of Baluchistan*. London: Society for Promoting Christian Knowledge.

Scoville, Thomas W. 1982. *Reorganizing for pacification support*. Washington, DC: Center of Military History. http://www.history.army.mil/books/Pacification_Spt (accessed 20 March 2013).

U.S. Senate. 2012. Testimony of General John R. Allen before the senate armed services committee, 20 March.

United States. The Pentagon Papers, Gravel Edition. *Chapter 2: The strategic hamlet program, 1961-1963.* Boston, MA: Beacon Press, 1971.

United States Agency for International Development (USAID). 2005. *USAID/Afghanistan strategic plan 2005-2010*. http://afghanistan.usaid.gov (accessed 13 January 2013).

———. 2010. USAID/Afghanistan country profile. http://afghanistan.usaid.gov (accessed 19 November 2012).

———. 2011a. USAID/Afghanistan interim report 2011. http://transition.usaid.gov, (accessed 21 November 2012).

———. 2011b. USAID Fact Sheet, Afghanistan social outreach program (ASOP). http://afghanistan.usaid.gov (accessed 13 January 2013).

U.S. Institute for Peace. 2009. *Guiding principles for stabilization and reconstruction*, Endowment of the United States Institute of Peace.

Younossi, Obaid. 2009. *The long march: Building an Afghan national army*. Arlington, VA: RAND Corporation.

Watteville, H. de. *Waziristan: 1919-1920*. Edited by Sir Callwell, Major General Charles. London Constable and Co. 1925.

White House. 2012. *Enduring strategic partnership agreement between the United States of America and the Islamic Republic of Afghanistan*. Washington DC: May.

White, Jeremy P. 2009. *Civil affairs in Vietnam*. Washington DC: Center for Strategic and International Studies. www.csis.org (accessed 2 April 2013).